JING SHEN

© Monkey Press, London, 2010
JING SHEN: the vital spirits, Huainanzi Chapter 7

ISBN 978 1 872468 10 5

www.monkeypress.net
info@monkeypress.net

Production and Design: Sandra Hill
Jing Shen calligraphy: Qu Lei Lei
Cover image: adapted from a tomb relief rubbing, Mixian, Henan Province.
Later Han Dynasty.

Printed by BookPress.eu

JING SHEN
THE VITAL SPIRITS
A translation of
HUAINANZI CHAPTER 7

Michelle Bromley, Deena Freeman
Alan Hext, Sandra Hill

under the aegis of
ELISABETH ROCHAT DE LA VALLÉE

MONKEY PRESS

PREFACE

Our group has been meeting for more than twenty years. The thrust of our work has been the joy of learning about translation from Chinese helped by our illustrious guides, and the insights we gain from the process of producing a translation paying scrupulous attention to the original Chinese characters and text.

The group was formed after an inspiring talk from Fr Claude Larre at a Traditional Acupuncture Society conference in Warwickshire in 1982. Elisabeth Rochat de la Vallée became involved as Fr Larre's assistant from early on, took on increasing responsibilities and became our formal tutor when Fr Larre died.

Membership was originally drawn from the acupuncture community. Our first work was on the Yellow Emperor's Inner Classic, (Nei Jing), but rapidly expanded to include the Daode Jing and then the Zhuangzi. Later we would venture to Liezi, Huainanzi, Guanzi and even find time for Confucius. The wider interest was reflected in a broader membership whose backgrounds included languages, sinology, music, banking, Buddhism, Daoism and just plain 'interested'. We have worked in Paris at the Institut Ricci, in Oxford, Cambridge and latterly in London, mostly by the river where we are soothed by the making and ebbing of the tide and the passing water traffic.

We worked on Huainanzi chapters 1 and 6, and when we came to 7, realized that no reliable English translation was available. Propitiously this chapter was also the subject of Fr Larre's doctoral thesis at the Sorbonne and the decision was made to prepare our own translation for publication. Now, some years on, it has been worked on by a skilled and diligent band of group members, and is deemed ready for the world.

The core phenomenon sustaining our group is the dedicated zeal with which Fr Larre and Elisabeth provide help with translation to folk who are not in the academic community, but who want to stick to rigorous standards and pay full regard to original texts. Their teaching is always done with elegance and a certain lightness.

So this text is dedicated to the memory of Father Claude Larre, to Elisabeth Rochat and to the continuation of the group.

Tim Gordon, London 2010

INTRODUCTION

Historical context

Jing Shen is the title of the seventh chapter of the Huainanzi, a major Daoist text of the early Chinese Han dynasty (206 BCE-221 CE). It bridges the time span from the earlier seminal texts of the Laozi and Zhuangzi to the Neo-daoist writings of the third and fourth century CE. Until recently the Huainanzi has remained relatively unrecognized and only partially translated. Long dismissed as merely a reiteration of earlier writings, its importance as a work in its own right and its role in Chinese intellectual history is only now beginning to be appreciated.

Its date is fairly well established; it was presented to the Emperor Wu Di by his uncle Liu An, Prince of Huainan, in 139 BCE in celebration of his accession to the throne. Illegitimate grandson of the founder of the Han dynasty, Liu An was a patron of learning and gathered scholars and literati at his court in Huainan (in present day Anhui province). It was here that the Huainanzi was composed – a collection of twenty essays, which range over the contemporary knowledge of cosmogony, metaphysics, ontology, mythology, geography, warfare and human conduct. The final essay, chapter 21, was written by Gao You, the great editor and commentator of the Huainanzi (168-212 CE), and provides a synoptic overview of the entire text.

Much of the material gathered together in the Huainanzi belongs, to the corpus of knowledge of previous generations, a large part of which had been lost or destroyed during the upheavals and repression of the Qin dynasty (221-206 BCE) and which was only extant in the memory of old scholars, embedded in their traditions and also retrieved through the discovery of hidden copies of texts. During this period of retrospection and reconstruction, there was an endeavour to gain a broader perspective of the past; and concomitant with that, an attitude of reverence and veneration for the wisdom of the sages of antiquity developed.

But the Huainanzi is much more than just an eclectic compendium of earlier knowledge. It draws on the philosophical ideas of the Laozhuang, yet distils and refines them, without diluting their provocative nature and thus preserving the wisdom that embraces the paradox of life. It contemplates their meaning, explores their implications, questions and elaborates on them in the context of contemporary human experience.

Numerology

Claude Larre always paid close attention to the significance of numerical ordering as a vital key to comprehending the unfolding meaning of the initial chapters of a Chinese classical text. Numerology is the hidden logic of heaven (nature, *tian* 天) manifesting on earth and within human beings as an integral ordering. This inner order can be seen in the early chapters of the Laozi, the Huangdi Neijing and also in the Huainanzi.

The first nine chapters of the Huainanzi present such an unfolding structure, the content of which sequentially reflect: 1. Dao at its source; 2. Looking beyond appearance; 3. Heaven; 4. Earth; 5. Seasonal regulation; 6. Mutual resonance; 7. The vital impulse of life in a human being; 8. Fundamental norm; 9. Rulership. Chapter seven therefore needs to be appreciated within this context. It is probable that the text was re-edited to reinforce this numerological interpretation.

At this time, numbers (*shu* 數) had not only a quantative value but a qualitative importance in Chinese culture. They reveal an awareness of the relationship of the One (*dao* 道) within the multiplicity at any given enumeration; the pairing of *yin yang* being the fundamental couple implicit within all even numbers.

Chapter seven explores the essential nature of a human being by way of the interplay of pairings, reflected emblematically in the couple of its title, *jing shen* (精 神). In common with all odd numbers, seven is the union emerging from the interaction of these couplings. In medical texts, seven is the number of the sensory orifices (two eyes, two ears, two nostrils, mouth) and also of the emotions (anger, elation, sadness, grief, obsessive thought, fear, fright) which, within a human being, may be stimulated by the information received by the sense organs. The odd enumeration can designate the awakening of life, but can also reflect disorder, for instance when emotions turn into destabilizing passions. Chapter seven frequently reflects upon this order/disorder, inner/outer, storing/dissipation in the life of a human being.

The structure of the chapter

Chapter seven of the Huainanzi, Jing Shen, vital or embodied spirit, examines the origins of life and the integral place of human beings within the cosmos. It begins with a description of the manifestation of life out of chaos, from formlessness to form, according to the patterning of the primal couple: 'Two spirits merged into life, to regulate heaven and organize earth', (lines 7-8).

In line 23, the human being emerges with the question: Within all this – 'How can "I" continue to exist?' The way the sage lives his life provides the answer: 'This is the reason why the sage adopts the model of heaven and follows his natural disposition' (lines 24-42). The model of heaven is illustrated by the generation of life described in Laozi chapter 42, and in the ordered growth seen in the nine months of human gestation, (lines 43-59). Human anatomy is perceived in mutual resonance with nature; human life as a perfect reflection of the cosmic order, (lines 60-83). The harmony or disharmony of human life depends on whether one is living in accordance with the *dao*, (lines 84-154). The individual then reflects, ponders and questions how he fits into the scheme of things, (lines 155-196). The final part of the text describes the way that the sages and authentic human beings live in harmony with the *dao*, (lines 196-300).

Our translation is only of the first part of the chapter; the latter part continues with a series of illustrations of this core text by means of stories and anecdotes.

Translation of the text and the textual notes

This book is presented in two sections – the first consisting of the Chinese text and translation, the second the textual notes. In the first section, the Chinese text is read according to the classical convention, from top to bottom, right to left; the characters are grouped to emphasize and delineate the inner structure and rhythm of the text. The English translation reflects the same structure; some of the text, where the rhythm is most apparent, appearing as verse, other sections in prose.

The textual notes take the text line by line, giving the Chinese, *pin yin* and English translation. Commentaries are added to explain various aspects of the translation, or to expand a point. Where a particularly medical theme is expressed, classical medical texts are referred to.

The translation faithfully follows the original text, but Chinese characters trigger a multitude of associations. For the most part, the translation maintains a consistency in the rendition of specific terms, but certain characters have been translated differently according to context. This is discussed in the textual notes.

Many of the Chinese phrases express meaning by their sound and rhythm in much the same way as concrete poetry, where the structure and meaning are one. The impenetrable vastness of the cosmos for example is expressed in the rhyming sonorities of *yao yao ming ming, hong men hong dong* (lines 3 and 5). This occurs again, in lines 31 and 32 where the relationship between heaven and earth is described by the characters *ding* and *qing* – 'earth is stable (*ding*), heaven is clear (*qing*)'. This use of rhythmical resonance can be seen clearly within the textual notes where the romanization in *pin yin* is given.

Certain characters, *dao* (道) and *de* (德), *yin* (陰) and *yang* (陽), *hun* (魂) and *po* (魄), have been left in the text as *pin yin*, as they refer to concepts which cannot be translated by a single English word. *Dao*, usually translated as the way, implies the way things are, the nature of things. In line 35 we see that 'emptiness and nothingness are the dwelling place of the *dao*.' Even though it is no-thing, non-being, it is nonetheless the source of all existence, the vital process in everything, and contains the potential of all that is, 'image without form' (line 2). *De* (often translated as power or virtue) is the creative function of the *dao*, the unfolding and manifestation of its potential. *Dao* is the state before manifestation, and the state to which all returns. *Yin* and *yang*, *hun* and *po* are further discussed below, and in the textual notes.

Jing Shen

The chapter title, Jing Shen, has usually been translated in the text as 'the vital spirits', though within a medical text it might more usually be seen as 'essences and spirits'. *Jing* is both adjective and noun, vital and vitality, essence and essential – it is the fundamental germ of life, the most subtle substance, the primordial stuff from which all life is made. In philosophical texts *jing* may represent pure vitality, a spiritual force. When combined with *shen*, spirits, it is life itself, the life-force, which can be seen in living beings through the light in the eyes, the shine of the hair, the texture of the skin. According to the cosmology of the early the Han dynasty, *jing* and *shen* may be seen as the expression of the natural and heavenly power of life, or as the merging of heavenly *shen* with the earthly *jing* that creates life within a human being. They represent the coming together of *yin* and *yang*, heaven and earth, space and time, to create life.

> '*Jing* is pure vitality, which gives rise to and permeates all forms on earth – it is a matrix for transformation; but it is also beyond form, the cosmic life-force. *Jing* is the foundation of all transformation and manifestation; the spirits (*shen*) give heavenly inspiration, allowing the heart to guide each individual towards their best possible natural fulfilment – their destiny (*ming* 命). The couple *jing shen* therefore expresses the origin, order and unfoldment of heaven and earth within a human being.'
> (Elisabeth Rochat de la Vallée)

Dynamic coupling

Life occurs when two complementary forces merge together, intertwine and act as one. All life is seen as a dynamic coupling, expressed in the text by *tian di* (天 地), heaven earth, *yin yang*, and specifically in the human being as *jing shen*. *Hun* (魂) and *po* (魄) are the couple that represent the two aspects of the human soul; death is their separation. The *hun* reflects *yang* and heaven, and returns at death to heaven; the *po* reflects *yin* and earth, and on death returns to the earth. As with the other couples referred to within the text, it is by their mutual penetration and intertwining that life is able to continue. 'Their *po* do not sink, their *hun* do not rise' (line 263) relates to the ability of the sage to hold this delicate balance of the qualities of *yin* and *yang* within body and soul.

The translators

In its contemplation of what it means to be an individual, suspended between the powers of heaven and earth, holding *yin* and *yang* in balance, this text was of particular interest to a group of lay translators, which includes many practitioners of Chinese medicine. We felt that our study of the contemporary Huangdi Neijing could throw some light on this enigmatic chapter, and allow us to give a unique slant to our translation. We originally worked on Huiananzi chapter 7 with Claude Larre in 1993, and many of his insights are reflected within the textual notes. As well as being indebted to the teaching of Claude Larre, more recently we have been guided by the scholarship and inspiration of Elisabeth Rochat de la Vallée. Elisabeth has shown untiring support and encouragement for our project, but although we have been dependent on her direction, the final translation is our own and we take responsibility for any errors. We have been constantly aware of Father Larre's attitude to translation, which is well expressed in his advisory remark: 'A translation has to be careful not to close the door on the possibilities of meaning.'

Since the original publication of the text, our friend and colleague Deena Freeman sadly died. We think of her whenever we open the book.

The edition of the text

The Chinese text is based on the edition of the Huainanzi by Liu Wendian (劉 文 典): Huai Nan Hong Lie Ji Jie (淮 南 鴻 烈 集 解), Shanghai, Shangwu, 1923; Taipei reprint, 1968. We read the annotations of Qing commentators, especially Wang Niansun (王 念 孫) and Yu Yue (俞 樾). Basically, the text used here is the edition adopted for the French translation by Fr. Claude Larre et E. Rochat de la Vallée, Le Cerf, Paris, 1993.

Quotations

Unless otherwise cited, translations are our own.

Michelle Bromley, Alan Hext, Sandra Hill,
London, 2010

Summary of Chapter Seven – from Chapter 21 of the Huainanzi

'"Jing Shen" – is the way to source the root where the life of a human being begins. It elucidates what enlivens their physical form and nine orifices. Receiving images from heaven, it equates their blood and *qi* with thunder and lightning, wind and rain; compares and classifies their joy and anger with light and darkness, cold and heat. It investigates the distinction between death and life; differentiates the traces of similarities and differences; and regulates the workings of movement and stillness, in order to return them to the ancestral origin of their innate nature and destiny. In this way, human beings may cherish and nourish their vital spirits, pacify and calm their *hun* and *po*, in order that things do not change themselves, and to maintain and protect that which dwells in emptiness and nothingness.'

精 神

JING SHEN:

THE VITAL SPIRITS

古未有天地之時

惟像無形

窈窈冥冥

芒芠漠閔

澒濛鴻洞

莫知其門

有二神混生

經天營地

孔乎

莫知其所終極

滔乎

莫知其所止息

於是乃

別為陰陽

離為八極

剛柔相成

萬物乃形

煩氣為蟲

精氣為人

In ancient times when heaven and earth did not yet exist
There was only image without form
> dark obscure
> formless soundless
> unfathomable profound

No-one knows its gate (1-6)

Two spirits merged into life
To regulate heaven and organize earth
Vast!
No-one knows how far they reach
Boundless!
No-one knows where they will stop and rest (7-12)

From this they divide into *yin yang*
Separate into eight poles
Hard and soft complete each other
And the ten thousand beings then take form
Coarse *qi* making insects
Subtle *qi* making humans (13-18)

4 • JING SHEN

是故精神天之有也
而骨骸者地之有也
精神入其門
而骨骸反其根
我尚何存

是故聖人法天順情
不拘於俗
不誘於人
以天為父
以地為母
陰陽為綱
四時為紀

天靜以清
地定以寧
失之者死
萬物法之者生

Therefore the vital spirits belong to heaven
And the bony frame belongs to earth
The vital spirits re-enter the gate
And the bony frame reverts to its root
How can 'I' continue to exist? (19-23)

This is the reason why the sage adopts the model of
        heaven and follows his natural disposition
He is not enticed by the worldly
He is not seduced by the human
He takes heaven as his father
He takes earth as his mother
Yin yang as guidelines
The four seasons as rules (24-30)

Heaven by its serenity is clear
Earth by its stability is tranquil
The ten thousand beings die by losing this
And live by taking it as their model (31-34)

夫靜漠者神明之定也

虛無者道之所居也

是故或求之於外者

有守之於內者

失之於外

譬猶本與末也

從本引之千枝萬葉莫不隨也

夫精神者所受於天也

而形體者所稟於地也

故曰一生二

二生三

三生萬物

萬物背陰而抱陽

沖氣以為和

In serenity and quietude, there settles the radiance of the
spirits
Emptiness and nothingness are the dwelling place of the *dao*
Therefore, the one who seeks it in the outside
                                    loses it on the inside
The one who keeps it on the inside
                                    loses it in the outside (35-38)

It is like root and branch
If it is pulled from the root the one thousand branches
            and ten thousand leaves cannot but follow (39-40)

It is the vital spirits that are received from heaven
And the body form that is provided by earth (41-42)

Thus it is said:
            one gives rise to two
            two gives rise to three
            three gives rise to the ten thousand beings
            the ten thousand beings lean on the *yin*
                        and embrace the *yang*
            and the powerful blending of *qi* makes harmony

                                                        (43-48)

故
曰

一月而膏
二月而胅
三月而胎
四月而肌
五月而筋
六月而骨
七月而成
八月而動
九月而躁
十月而生
形體以成
五藏乃形

是故
肺主目
腎主鼻
膽主口
肝主耳
外為表
而內為裏

開閉張歙
各有經紀也
故頭之圓也象天
足之方也象地

Therefore it is said:

> at one month it is a rich paste
> at two months it is a bulge
> at three months it is a foetus
> at four months it has flesh
> at five months it has sinews
> at six months it has bones
> at seven months it is complete
> at eight months it moves
> at nine months it quickens
> at ten months it is born (49-59)

As the body form becomes complete
The five organs then take form (60-61)

For this reason the lungs master the eyes
The kidneys master the nose
The gallbladder masters the mouth
The liver masters the ears
The outer are for external expression
And the internal are for inner organization (62-67)

Opening and closing, expanding and contracting
Each has its regulations and rules
Thus the roundness of the head is in the image of heaven
The square made by the feet is in the image of earth (68-71)

天有四時五行九解三百六十六日

人亦有四支五藏九竅三百六十六節

人亦有風雨寒暑

人亦有取與喜怒

故膽為雲

肺為氣

肝為風

腎為雨

脾為雷

以與天地相參也而心為之主

是故耳目者日月也

血氣者風雨也

而

日中有踆鳥

月中有蟾蜍

日月失其行

薄蝕無其光

風雨非其時

毀折生其災

五星失其行

州國受殃

Heaven has four seasons, five moving forces, nine releasings and 366 days; human beings similarly have four
limbs, five organs, nine orifices and 366 articulations.
Heaven has wind and rain, cold and heat; human beings
similarly have taking and giving, joy and anger. (72-75)

Therefore the gallbladder makes clouds
>the lungs *qi*
>the liver wind
>the kidneys rain
>the spleen thunder

There is mutual participation with heaven and earth
>and the heart is master

That is why ear and eye are sun and moon
Blood and *qi* are wind and rain (76-83)

In the centre of the sun there is a three-legged crow
And in the middle of the moon there is a spotted toad
When sun and moon lose their course
They catch and devour each other and there is no light
When wind and rain are not in season
They wreak havoc and bring about disaster
When the five planets lose their course
The regions and states suffer catastrophe (84-91)

夫天地之道至紘以大
尚猶節其章光愛其神
明

人之耳目曷能久熏勞而不息乎
精神何能久馳騁而不既乎
是故血氣者人之華也而五藏者人之精也

夫血氣能專於五藏而不外越則胸腹充而嗜欲省矣
胸腹充而嗜欲省則耳目清聽視達矣
耳目清聽視達謂之明

The *dao* of heaven and earth by its ultimate immensity is
great
Yet it moderates its display of light and cares for the
radiance of the spirits (92-93)

How can the ears and the eyes of man work long and
hard without rest?
How can the vital spirits race fast and furious without
exhaustion?
For this reason blood and *qi* are the splendour of man and
the five organs are his essences (94-96)

When blood and *qi* are concentrated in the five organs
and not dispersed outside,
then chest and abdomen are replete, longing and desire
diminish
When chest and abdomen are replete, and longing and
desires diminished,
then ears and eyes are clear, hearing and seeing acute
When ears and eyes are clear, hearing and seeing acute,
that is called illumination (97-102)

五藏能屬於心而無乖
則教志勝而行之不僻矣
則教志勝而行之不僻
則神盛而氣不散矣
精神盛而氣不散則理
　　　　　　理則均
　　　　　　均則通
　　　　　　通則神
　　　　神則
　　　　以視無不見也
　　　　以聽無不聞也
　　　　以為無不成也
　　是故憂患不能入也而邪氣不能襲
　　故事有求之於四海之外而不能遇
　　故或守之於形骸之內而不見也
故所求多者所得少
所見大者所知小

When the five organs are able to submit to the heart
without resistance, then however powerful the rising
of the will, the behaviour does not deviate. However
powerful the rising of the will, if the behaviour does not
deviate, then the vital spirits thrive and the *qi* are not
scattered. When the vital spirits thrive and the *qi* are not
scattered, then there is perfect order. (103-107)

> perfect order, then equilibrium
> equilibrium, then free communication
> free communication, then the spirits (108-110)

With the spirits

> in looking there is nothing that is not seen
> in listening there is nothing that is not heard
> in doing there is nothing that is not accomplished
> (111-114)

Thus worries and concerns cannot enter and perverse *qi*
cannot strike
Though actively seeking it beyond the four seas it cannot
be found
And guarding it within the physical form it cannot be seen
Therefore, those who seek too much gain less
Those who look for the great know little (115-119)

夫孔竅者精神之戶牖也

而氣志者五藏之使候也

耳目淫於聲色之樂

則五藏搖動而不定矣

五藏搖動而不定

則血氣滔蕩而不休矣

則血氣滔蕩而不休

則精神馳騁於外而不守矣

則精神馳騁於外而不守

則禍福之至雖如丘山無由識之矣

Openings and orifices are the windows and doors of the
vital spirits
And *qi* and will are the messengers and stewards of the
five organs
When ears and eyes are corrupted by the pleasures of
sounds and colours,
then the five organs are shaken and rattled and have no
stability (120-123)

When the five organs, shaken and rattled, have no
stability,
then blood and *qi* overflow recklessly and do not settle
When the blood and *qi* overflow recklessly and do not
settle,
then the vital spirits race fast and furious out of bounds
and are not contained
When the vital spirits race fast and furious out of bounds
and are not contained,
then even if good or bad fortune were as imposing as a
mountain, there would be no way of recognizing them for
what they are (124-129)

使耳目精明玄達而無誘慕
氣志虛靜恬愉而省嗜欲
五藏定寧充盈而不泄
精神內守形骸而不外越
則望於往世之前而視於來事之後

猶未足為也
豈直禍福之間哉
故曰其出彌遠者其知彌少
以言夫精神之不可使外淫也

是故
五色亂目使目不明
五聲譁耳使耳不聰
五味亂口使口爽傷
趣舍滑心使行飛揚
此四者天下之所養性也然皆人累也

If ear and eye are vital and bright, deep and penetrating, and do not yearn or covet; if *qi* and will are empty and serene, calm and content, and longings and desires diminish; if the five organs are stable and tranquil, satisfied and replete, and nothing leaks away; if the vital spirits are contained within the physical form, and are not dispersed outside – then the vision extends beyond what came before the past and reaches to what is after the future. (130-134)

Even that is not enough!
So how is it possible to distinguish between good and bad fortune?
It is said: 'the further one goes the less one knows'
This means that one should not allow the vital spirits to move outward and degenerate (135-138)

So, when the five colours confuse the eye, the eye cannot see clearly. When the five sounds deafen the ear, the ear cannot hear acutely. When the five tastes confuse the mouth, the palate is spoiled. When attractions and aversions trouble the heart, actions fly astray. By these four, all under heaven nourish their innate nature, only human beings become bound. (139-143)

故曰嗜欲者使人之氣越
而好憎者使人之心勞
弗疾去則志氣日耗

夫人之所以不能終其壽命而中道夭於刑戮者何也
以其生之厚
夫惟能無以生為者則所以脩得生也

夫天地運而相通萬物總而為一
能知一則無一之不知也
不能知一則無一之能知也

譬吾處於天下也亦為一物矣不識天下之以我備其物與
且惟無我而物無不備者乎
然則我亦物也
物之與物也
又何以相物也

So it is said:
Longing and desire cause the *qi* of man to be dispersed,
and liking and loathing cause the heart of man to be
weary. If they are not immediately expelled, then will and
qi deteriorate day by day. (144-146)

Why are men unable to reach the end of their given lifespan
but die young midway, through punishment or execution?
It is because they live their life too fully. Only those who
do not live for life obtain long life. (147-150)

So heaven and earth revolve in mutual exchange,
and the ten thousand beings altogether make the One.
For those able to know the One – nothing is unknown.
For those unable to know the One – nothing can be known.
(151-154)

If we consider our place in the world, it is the place of one
being. I do not know whether the world completes its collection of beings through me, or whether its collection of
beings would still be complete without me. Indeed I am
also a being. A being amongst beings. Beings in relation
to other beings. How can beings be distinguished from
one another? (155-162)

雖然

其生我也將以何益

其殺我也將以何損

夫造化者既以我為坯矣

將無所違之矣

吾安知夫刺灸而欲生者之非惑也

又安知夫絞經而求死者之非福也

或者生乃徭役也

而死乃休息也

天下茫茫孰知之哉

其生我也不彊求已

其殺我也不彊求止

欲生而不事

憎死而弗辭

賤之而弗憎

貴之而弗喜

隨其天資而安之不極

Even so

What gain is there for giving me life?

What loss for taking my life away? (163-165)

That which produces and transforms moulds me like clay

I would have no reason to resist

How can we know if the one who has needles and moxa

in the desire to live, is not deluded?

How can we know if the one who ties a cord around his

neck seeking death, is not fortunate?

Perhaps life is just forced labour

and death just rest (166-171)

The world is vast and wide – how can it be known?

Life is given to me – I do not try to end it

Life is taken from me – I do not try to stop it

I desire life – but make nothing of it

I loathe death – but do not refuse it

Being lowly – I do not loathe it

Being noble – I do not rejoice in it

I follow the disposition of heaven and content in this,

do not push beyond (172-179)

吾生也有七尺之形

吾死也有一棺之土

吾生之比於有形之類

吾死之淪於無形之中也

猶

然則吾生也物不以益眾

吾死也土不以加厚

吾又安知所喜憎利害其間者乎

夫造化者之攫援物也譬猶陶人之埏埴也

其取之地而已為盆盎也與其未離於地也無以異

其已成器而破碎漫瀾而復歸其故也

與其為盆盎亦無以異矣

In life we have a body of seven feet
In death we occupy one coffin in the earth
In life we belong to the category of what has form
In death we are engulfed in the midst of the formless
(180-183)

So, alive, we do not increase the multitude of beings
Dead, we do not add to the thickness of the earth
How could I know the difference between joy and
loathing, benefit and harm? (184-186)

Now, that which produces and transforms takes hold
of a being as a potter works clay. The clay taken from
the earth and shaped into a bowl or dish is no different
from the clay which is not yet separated from the earth.
Having become a utensil it will be shattered in small
pieces, dispersed and dissolved and return to its former
state. Compared to when it was a bowl or dish, there is no
difference. (187-191)

夫臨江之鄉居人汲水以浸其園江水弗憎也

苦洿之家決洿而注之江洿水弗樂也

是故其在江也亦無以異其在江也

是故聖人

因時以安其位

當世而樂其業

夫悲樂者德之邪也

而喜怒者道之過也

好憎者心之暴也

故曰

其生也天行

其死也物化

靜則與陰俱閉

動則與陽俱開

精神澹然無極

不與物散

而天下自服

Now, in the villages by the river, they draw water to soak their gardens; the water from the river feels no resentment. Families plagued by stagnant water open a passage for it to flow into the river; the stagnant water feels no pleasure. This is because the water from the river is no different from the water soaking the gardens. In the same way the stagnant water is no different from the water in the river. (192-195)

Therefore the sage:
Following the appropriate time is content in his position
Adapting to the age takes pleasure in his activities
Sadness and happiness are perversions of the *de*
And joy and anger are deviations from the *dao*
Likes and dislikes do violence to the heart
Therefore it is said:

> 'His life is a movement of heaven,
> His death a transformation of things
> In stillness he shares the closing of the *yin*
> In motion he shares the opening of the *yang*'

(196-205)

His vital spirits being calm are without limit
He does not let himself be dissipated by beings
And all under heaven naturally yield to him (206-208)

故心者形之主也

而神者心之寶也

形勞而不休則蹶

精用而不已則竭

是故聖人貴

而尊之不敢越也

夫有夏后氏之璜者匣匱而藏之寶之至也

夫精神之可寶也非直夏后氏之璜也

是故聖人以無應有必究其理

以虛受實必窮其節

恬愉虛靜以終其命

是故無所甚疏而無所甚親

抱德煬和以順于天

與道為際與德為鄰

不為福始

不為禍先

魂魄處其宅而精神守其根

死生無變於己故曰至神

所謂真人者性合于道也

Thus the heart is the master of the body, and the spirits the treasure of the heart. The body labouring without rest collapses, essences used unceasingly run dry. Therefore the sage appreciates and values them, and does not dare abuse them. (209-212)

The semicircular jade of Xia Hou is stored in a secure box because it is a treasure of the utmost value. Now, are not the essences and spirits more precious than the semicircular jade of Xia Hou? Therefore the sage responds to what is by means of what is not and so penetrates its inner principle. By means of emptiness he receives its fullness and so fathoms its rhythms. Calm and content, empty and still, he fulfils his destiny. (213-217)

Therefore, nothing is very distant from him, nothing is very close. Embracing the *de*, merging harmoniously, he follows heaven. Side by side with the *dao*, neighbours with the *de*, he does not make good fortune his premise nor bad fortune his precedent. *Hun* and *po* keep their places and the vital spirits guard his root. For him life and death are not a change, therefore he is called a perfect spirit. To be called an authentic man means that his nature unites with the *dao*. (218-224)

故有而若無
實而若虛

處其一不知其二
治其內不識其外
明白太素無為復樸
體本抱神

以游于天地之樊芒然彷徉于塵垢之外而消搖于無事之業

浩浩蕩蕩乎

機械知巧弗載於心
是故死生亦大矣而不為變
雖天地覆育亦不與之捃抱矣
審乎無瑕而不與物糅
見事之亂而能守其宗

Therefore, being is the same as not being
Fullness is the same as emptiness (225-226)

Dwelling in oneness he does not know the two
Absorbed in the interior he pays no attention to the exterior
In pure illumination, great simplicity and non-doing
he returns to the uncarved block
He embodies the origin and embraces spirit (227-230)

Roaming in the enclosure of heaven and earth, wandering
obliviously to and fro beyond the dusty world, and
ambling about occupied with non-activity. (231)

Vast! Boundless! (232)

Cleverness and skilfulness do not burden his heart.
Therefore death and life are of equal importance and
neither is a change. Although heaven covers him and
earth nurtures him, he does not cling to them. He
scrutinizes the flawless and does not get mixed up with
things. Perceiving the confusion of worldly affairs he is
still able to preserve his ancestral origin. (233-237)

若然者忘肝膽遺耳目
心志專于內通達耦于一

居不知所為行不知所之渾然而往逯然而來

形若槁木心若死灰

忘其五藏損其形骸

不學而知不視而見

不為而成不治而辯

不感而應迫而動

不得已而往如光之燿如景之放

以道為紃有待而然

抱其太清之本而無所容與而物無能營

廓惝而虛清靖而無思慮

Men like that forget their liver and gall, neglect their ears and eyes, and with their heart and will concentrated within, their penetration and comprehension make them companions with the One. (238-239)

Staying still, they do not know what they are doing, on the move they do not know where they are going; chaotically they go and randomly they come. Their bodies are like dried wood, their hearts are like dead ashes. Having forgotten their five organs and destroyed their physical form, they do not study yet they know; they do not look, yet they see; they do not act, yet they accomplish; they do not rule, yet they govern. They respond when stimulated, they move when pushed. They cannot help but go aimlessly as a ray of light, like shadows cast. (240-246)

They take the *dao* as their law, awaiting its cue. They embrace the root of the great purity and are not concerned with anyone, so nothing can trouble them. Expansive, vast and empty! Pure, tranquil and without thoughts and cares. (247-249)

大澤焚而不能熱也

大河漢涸而不能寒也

大雷毀山而不能驚也

大風晦日而不能傷也

是故視珍寶珠玉猶石礫也

視至尊窮寵猶行客也

視毛嬙西施猶顙醜也

以死生為一化

以萬物為一方

同精於太清之本而游於忽區之旁

有精而不使有神而不行

契大渾之樸而立至清之中

是故其寢不夢其智不萌

故其魄不抑其魂不騰

Huge marshes set alight cannot burn them; rivers and streams ice over but cannot freeze them; great thunder storms break down mountains but cannot frighten them; great winds obscure the sun but cannot harm them. (250-253)

Therefore they consider jewels such as pearls and jade as if they were gravel. They regard the highest dignitaries and those most favoured as travellers at the door. They consider Mao Qiang and Xi Shi as ugly and deformed. They regard death and life as transformations within the One and the ten thousand beings as an aspect of the One. (254-258)

They share essences with the root of the great purity, they roam about in the region of the indistinct. They have essences but do not use them, they have spirits but do not activate them. They have a pact with the primal simplicity of the great chaos and they stand in the centre of the perfect purity. Therefore their sleep is without dreams; their wisdom does not burst forth; their *po* do not sink and their *hun* do not rise. (259-263)

反
覆
終
始
不
知
其
端
緒

甘
瞑
太
宵
之
宅

而
覺
視
于
昭
昭
之
宇

休
息
于
無
委
曲
之
隅

而
游
敖
于
無
形
埒
之
野

居
而
無
容
處
而
無
所

其
動
若
無
形
其
靜
若
無
體

存
而
若
亡
生
而
若
死

出
入
無
間
役
使
鬼
神

淪
於
不
測
入
於
無
間
以
不
同
形
相
嬗
也

終
始
若
環
莫
得
其
倫

此
精
神
之
所
以
能
登
假
於
道
也

They go back and forth between beginnings and endings
not knowing their extremities and the successions
They delight in closing their eyes in the abode of the great
night and they awaken and look around in the house of
the brilliant light
They rest and relax in a cornerless corner
And roam to and fro in a wilderness without form (264-268)

They dwell in a space that cannot contain, settle in a place
that is nowhere; they move in the formless; are still in the
bodyless
They are present as if vanished and live as if dead
They enter and leave where there is no opening, use
ghosts and spirits as servants
They are engulfed by the unfathomable and enter into
what has no opening, in order to be moulded into
different forms
Endings and beginnings are like a circle, no-one can grasp
their succssion
This is how the vital spirits are able to merge with the *dao*
(269-275)

是故真人之所游若吹呴呼吸吐故內新
熊經鳥伸鳧浴蝯躩鴟視虎顧
是養形之人也
不以滑心

使神滔蕩而不失其充
日夜無傷而與物為春
則是合而生時於心也

且人有戒形而無損於心
有綴宅而無耗精
夫癲者趨不變狂者形不虧
神將有所遠徙孰知其所為

故形有摩而神未嘗化者
以不化應化
千變萬抮而未始有極

Therefore, the authentic men in their roamings do not let their hearts be disturbed by puffing and blowing, inhaling and exhaling, expelling the old, taking in the new; bear lumbering, bird stretching, duck ablutions, monkey jumping, owl gazing and tiger staring – all that is for men to nourish the body. (276-279)

Even if they use their spirits until they overflow, they do not lose their fullness. They are unharmed day and night and are spring for beings. Then there is unity and timeliness is generated in the heart. (280-282)

The human body is prepared and the heart is not weakened. From dwelling place to dwelling place, the essences are not exhausted. The leper's pace is not changed by his disease and the body of a madman is not impaired. But if their spirits flee far away who knows what will happen? (283-286)

So the body wears out, but the spirits are not subject to transformation. Because they are not transformed, they resonate with all transformations. A thousand changes and ten thousand twists and turns – and not even the beginning of their limit. (287-289)

化者復歸於無形也
不化者與天地俱生也

夫木之死也青青去之也
夫使木生者豈木也其所生則死矣
猶充形者之非形也其所化則化矣
故生生者未嘗死也其所化則化矣
化物者未嘗化也

輕天下則神無累矣
細萬物則心不惑矣
齊死生則志不懾矣
同變化則明不眩矣

That which is transformed returns and reverts to the formless. That which is not transformed shares all life with heaven and earth. (290-291)

A tree dies when the green vitality departs. So how could it be that what makes a tree alive is the tree itself? In the same way, what gives the body its fullness is not the body itself. Therefore, that which generates life never dies, but that which is given life dies. That which transforms beings is never transformed; it is that which is transformed which is transformed. (292-296)

Giving no importance to the world, the spirits are not entangled
Making little of the ten thousand beings, the heart is not deluded
Considering life and death as equal, the will is not shaken
Regarding all change and transformation as the same, clarity is not obscured (297-300)

精 神

JING SHEN

TEXTUAL NOTES

1. 古 未 有 天 地 之 時
gu wei you tian di zhi shi
In ancient times when heaven and earth did not yet exist

The first line of Huainanzi chapter 7 is similar to that of Huainanzi chapter 3, and both are derived from the opening line of the chapter Tianwen of the Chuci, the Songs of Chu:

> 'In the beginning of old, all is yet formless, no up or down.
> Dark and light are a blur, the only image is a whir.'
> (J. S. Major)

It is also a reference to Zhuangzi chapter 6: 'In the time before heaven and earth', and suggests that this is less a temporal indication than a representation of the *dao* itself, or of the 'One' before any division occurred.

2. 惟 像 無 形
wei xiang wu xing
There was only image without form

Xiang (象) is a model or patterning for the process whereby life comes into being, as *dao* manifests itself. Its first appearance in chapter seven of the Huainanzi has the radical for 'human' added (像), which gives the character the connotation of a living manifestation. In the Xici, the great commentary to the Yijing, the *si xiang* (四 象), four images, appear as the model for the organization of life.

This idea of image without form is found in Laozi chapter 41: *da xiang wu xing* (大 象 無 形) the great image is without form. *Xiang* contains the potential of all phenomena not yet expressed. It exhibits no particularity, and is at the level 'before heaven and earth'.

3. 窈 窈 冥 冥
yao yao ming ming
dark obscure

These characters are used to give an atmospheric impression of the origin, which is evoked by the repetition and the rhythmical nature of the phrasing. This section of the Huainanzi attempts to put into words something that is very elusive and evasive.

The character *yao* (窈) is capped by the radical *xue* (穴) which is a hollowed out cavern, the term also used for an acupuncture point. *Ming* (冥) is capped by the radical *mi,* (冖) to cover. Together they give the meaning of concealed forces hidden underground.

4 芒 芠 漠 閔
mang wen mo min
formless soundless

5. 澒 濛 鴻 洞
hong meng hong dong
unfathomable profound

Similarly, all four characters *hong meng hong dong* (澒 濛 鴻 洞) have the water radical. In *hong* it is the imperceptible penetration of water which has no limit. The flowing movement of running water is seen as the first virtue that manifests after heaven and earth are formed.

6. 莫 知 其 門
mo zhi qi men
No-one knows its gate
This is the gate between form and formless, existing and not existing. Where there is no gate there is no entry.

cf: Laozi chapter 6:
> 'The spirit of the valley never dies
> It is called the dark feminine
> The gate of the dark feminine
> Is called the root of heaven and earth'

cf: Huainanzi chapter 1:
> 'The convergence of the myriad things
> Goes through a single aperture;
> The roots of the various happenings
> All issue forth from a single gateway.
> Its movements are hidden from sight.' (Ames and Lau)

7. 有 二 神 混 生
you er shen hun sheng
Two spirits merged into life

You er (有 二), to be two, is used in contrast to the earlier *wu xing* (無 形), to have no form, no body, to be formless. *You* (有) implies to be alive. The two spirits are born yet they still intermingle with chaos (*hun* 混). Hun is to be chaotic, mixed together, and is part of the expression *hun tun* (混 吞).

cf: Laozi chapter 25:
> 'There was something formed out of chaos
> That was born before Heaven and Earth.
> Quiet and still! Pure and deep!' (R. B. Hendricks)

The spirits represent the possibility of life. They may be symbolized by the legendary Fuxi and Nugua – the two principles of the manifestation of life on earth.

> 'The *taiji* (太極, supreme pole) produces the two principles. These two principles produce the four images. The four images produce the eight trigrams.' (Xici 1, 11)

8. 經 天 營 地
　jing tian ying di
To regulate heaven and organize earth

Fuxi and Nugua regulate (*jing* 經) heaven and organize (*ying* 營) earth
with their compass and square. The compass symbolizes the circle of
heaven and the succession of time; the square represents the earth, and
thus space and location. (cf: lines 70-71)

Fuxi and Nugua

Jing and *ying* can be interpreted as to measure, to order, to plan, to
design. In Chinese medicine, *jing* is the organization of the meridian
system; *ying* the structuration possible from nutrition.

cf: Shijing, Jingying Sifang (經 營 四 方): the regulation,
organization and disposition of the four quarters of the empire.

9. 孔 乎
　kong hu
Vast!
Here again the resonant sound of the character *kong* (孔) suggests an
echoing vastness, it has the meaning of an opening through which *qi*
blows forth to animate the ten thousand things.

10. 莫 知 其 所 終 極
mo zhi qi suo zhong ji
No-one knows how far they reach

The transformative power of the two spirits has no limit. In this text *ji* (極) is translated as limit, extremity. There is nothing beyond; it is the supreme limit, the ridgepole.

11. 滔 乎
tao hu
Boundless!

12. 莫 知 其 所 止 息
mo zhi qi suo zhi xi
No-one knows where they will stop and rest

13. 於 是 乃 別 為 陰 陽
yu shi nai bie wei yin yang
From this they divide into *yin yang*

The two spirits (*er shen* 二 神), are an undifferentiated unity (chaos, *hun* 混). But *yin yang* are the One manifesting at the level of the two, and are therefore distinguishable. The separation into *yin* and *yang* is also the differentiation of heaven and earth, the light diffusing to become heaven, the dark and dense condensing to form earth.

cf: Huainanzi chapter 3:
    'A shoreline divides the primordial *qi*
    That which is pure and bright spreads out to form heaven
    The heavy and turbid congeals to form earth.' (J. S. Major)

cf: Neijing Suwen chapter 5:
    'The accumulation of *yang* is heaven,
    The accumulation of *yin* is earth.'

Bie (別) is the function of distinction, which allows a continual inter-penetration, and thereby a fruitful relationship. *Yin* and *yang* exist only with and within each other.

14. 離 為 八 極
    li wei ba ji
Separate into eight poles

Li (離) is the name of the trigram fire, which contains the ability to separate and discriminate. The further separation of *yin* and *yang* creates the eight poles. The eight poles represent the eight directions and the eight winds, which circulate and harmonize the *qi* from the eight directions of space. They are also linked historically with the eight trigrams. Here *ji* (極) is translated as pole – but can also be understood as extreme, limitless (see note to line 10).

15. 剛 柔 相 成
    gang ruo xiang cheng
Hard and soft complete each other

Hard and soft form one of the primary *yin yang* distinctions, also seen in the complete (–) and broken (--) lines of the Yijing hexagrams. The dynamic of the couple is fundamental and intrinsic to the subsequent expansion of life. The hard and the soft are also understood as sexual intercourse from which all forms of life come into being. *Cheng* (成) is the materialization and the accomplishment of form. Hard (*gang* 剛) and soft (*ruo* 柔) complement or complete each other. In the human body this may be seen as bones and flesh.

16. 萬 物 乃 形
wan wu nai xing
And the ten thousand beings then take form

The ten thousand beings represent all possible manifestation. Once hard and soft complete each other all beings can take form (*xing* 形) and achieve completion. This is the fulfilment of the two spirits mentioned above.

17. 煩 氣 為 蟲
fan qi wei chong
Coarse *qi* making insects

18. 精 氣 為 人
jing qi wei ren
Subtle *qi* making humans

Fan qi, coarse *qi,* suggest a lesser quality of *qi.* Here it is contrasted with *jing qi* (精 氣), the light, subtle and essential *qi* natural to human beings. It is this essential subtlety of human beings which allows the development of the vital spirits (*jing shen*).

The earliest meaning of the character *jing* is the most subtle, refined and nutritious flour, which is often contrasted with a coarse flour which is not easily assimilated.

19. 是 故 精 神 天 之 有 也
shi gu jing shen tian zhi you ye
Therefore the vital spirits belong to heaven

This is the first reference in the text of Huainanzi chapter 7 to the *jing shen* (精 神) of the title. Within the classical medical texts, *jing* generally refers to the most pure and refined aspects of the material;

it is the substratum of refined essences needed to attract and hold the more ethereal *shen*. The *shen* allows the sequential development of life through transformation. *Jing* gives features and form. Together *jing shen* suggest the life-force in its *yin yang* intertwining. Here in Huainanzi chapter 7, *jing* is mostly used to express the vitality of the spirits *(shen)*of heaven and their manifestation within a human being.

In the Chinese concept of vitality, body and spirit are inseparable. Clarity of vision, for example, refers equally to the physical mechanism of the eyes as to the interpretation of what is seen. The combination and collaboration of vital essences and spirits (*jing shen* 精 神) allows perfect functioning of body and mind.

20. 而 骨 骸 者 地 之 有 也
    er gu hai zhe di zhi you ye
And the bony frame belongs to earth

The bony frame refers to the bodily form. When buried, it is only the bones that remain in the earth.

21. 精 神 入 其 門
    jing shen ru qi men
The vital spirits re-enter the gate

This is the separation at death of what descends back into the earth and what returns to heaven.

cf: Wang Bi's commentary to Laozi chapter 10:

> '"The gateway of Heaven" is a term for that through which all under Heaven passes…' (R. J. Lynn)

22. 而 骨 骸 反 其 根
    er gu hai fan qi gen
And the bony frame reverts to its root

Its root is the earth. Lines 19-22 describe a vision of the One
manifesting itself, as life comes into being, and then separates at
death.

23. 我 尚 何 存
    wo shang he cun
How can 'I' continue to exist?

I, (*wo* 我), am simply the result of *yin yang,* the interpenetration of
heaven and earth. At death they separate and I no longer exist as a
living being. My destiny is to allow what belongs to earth (the bony
frame) to return to earth and what belongs to heaven (the vital spirits)
to re-enter the gate.

24. 是 故 聖 人 法 天 順 情
    shi gu sheng ren fa tian shun qing
**This is the reason why the sage adopts the model of heaven and
follows his natural disposition**

Qing (情) is the natural disposition, which flourishes when following
the model of heaven or the natural order. But *qing* is also emotion, and
if the human heart/mind is not in alignment with the model of heaven,
there arise attractions, repulsions and even desires.

cf: Laozi chapter 25 where adopting the model of heaven allows a
return to nature's spontaneity, to what is so by itself (*ziran* 自 然).

  'Man models himself on earth,
  Earth on heaven,

Heaven on the way,
And the way on that which is naturally so (*ziran*).' (D. C. Lau)

25. 不 拘 於 俗
bu ju yu su
He is not enticed by the worldly

26. 不 誘 於 人
bu you yu ren
He is not seduced by the human

If *qing* (情) is the natural disposition which exists within us before the expression of emotion, *su* (俗) refers to the earthly part of life, to customs and day to day preoccupations. In this context, to be human is the capacity to oppose heaven, to go against the natural order. *Su* can be translated as vulgar or common, but here refers to social customs, which may be good or bad depending on the context and the way they are applied. Customs are behavioural patterns devised within human society and may be contrary to the natural order of life.

cf: Huainanzi chapter 1, Section 10 (see Ames and Lau)

27. 以 天 為 父
yi tian wei fu
He takes heaven as his father

28. 以 地 為 母
yi di wei mu
He takes earth as his mother

29. 陰 陽 為 綱
yin yang wei gang
Yin yang as guidelines

30. 四 時 為 紀
si shi wei ji
The four seasons as rules

Yin and *yang* are the guiding principles (great law) and the four seasons
their multiplication, the various rules and regulations, manifesting
as the interaction of heaven upon earth. The character *gang* (綱),
translated here as guidelines, is the image of the main rope of a net that
can gather everything in. It could be translated as both principle and
principal. *Ji* (紀) is the fine mesh, the net that can catch the smallest
fish, and hence implies the regulation of the finest details of life.

cf: Neijing Suwen chapter 5:
'*Yin yang* is the way of heaven and earth, the great law (*gang*
綱) and rules (*ji* 紀) of the 10,000 beings, father and mother of
change and transformation, origin and beginning of life and death,
residence of the radiance of the spirits (*shen ming* 神 明).'

31. 天 靜 以 清
tian jing yi qing
Heaven by its serenity (*jing* 靜) is clear (*qing* 清)

32. 地 定 以 寧
di ding yi ning
Earth by its stability (*ding* 定) is tranquil (*ning* 寧)

There is a musical resonance in the Chinese description of the qualities
of heaven and earth. *Jing,* serenity and *qing,* clarity have a lighter

sonority. *Ding*, stability and *ning*, tranquillity, have a heavier sonority. These four terms are used extensively within daoist meditative texts to suggest the stillness of the mind and stability of the body.

cf: Laozi chapter 39:
    'Heaven by attaining the One becomes clear (*qing* 清),
    Earth by attaining the One becomes tranquil (*ning* 寧).'

33. 萬 物 失 之 者 死
    wan wu shi zhi zhe si
The ten thousand beings die by losing this

34. 法 之 者 生
    fa zhi zhe sheng
And live by taking it as their model (*fa* 法)

35. 夫 靜 漠 者 神 明 之 定 也
    fu jing mo zhe shen ming zhi ding ye
In serenity and quietude, there settles the radiance of the spirits.

When applied to the inner life, the character *mo* (漠) means silence, solitude, calm, but it can also mean impartiality. The state of quietude is beyond differentiation, providing an abode for the radiant spirits (*shen ming* 神 明). *Shen ming* is the radiant luminosity which emanates from the presence of the spirits.

'*Shen ming* is also a clear and pure mind, spiritual intelligence, a mind capable of penetrating the reality of the cosmos, as well as the reality of an individual human life. It is also the pure functioning of vitality within the body, perfect health.' (E. Rochat de la Vallée)

36. 虛 無 者 道 之 所 居 也
xu wu zhe dao zhi suo ju ye

Emptiness (*xu* 虛) and nothingness (*wu* 無) are the dwelling place of the *dao*

Xu wu (虛 無) suggests absolute emptiness, the void. It is full of all potentiality as yet unmanifested. The sage is willing to welcome the *shen ming* (神 明), the radiance of the spirits, and to dwell in the absolute emptiness of the *dao*. The sage has no preferences, no personal ideas or images in the heart, but goes along with the spirit of heaven and is at one with all change and transformation.

cf: Laozi chapter 49:
  'The sage has no fixed mind' (E. Ryden)

cf: Zhuangzi chapter 6:
  'This is what I call not using the mind to repel the way...'
  (B. Watson)

37. 是 故 或 求 之 於 外 者 失 之 於 內
shi gu huo qiu zhi yu wai zhe shi zhi yu nei

Therefore, the one who seeks it in the outside, loses it on the inside

38. 有 守 之 於 內 者 失 之 於 外
you shou zhi yu nei zhe shi zhi yu wai

The one who keeps it on the inside, loses it in the outside.

Nei (內) suggests what is essential and fundamental; *wai* (外) what is secondary and superficial. Together, they are another expression of *yinyang* counterbalance: interior and exterior, within and without, permanent and transitory, the essential and the incidental, the central and the peripheral. (cf: lines 66 and 67)

39. 譬猶本與末也
pi you ben yu mo ye
It is like root and branch

40. 從本引之千枝萬葉莫不隨也
cong ben yin zhi qian zhi wan ye mo bu sui ye
**If it is pulled from the root the one thousand branches and ten
thousand leaves cannot but follow** (*sui* 隨)

The double negative *mo bu* (莫 不) is used as an emphatic – the
ten thousand leaves cannot not follow. Sui (隨), to follow, is the
compliance seen in the name of hexagram 17 of the Yijing.

41. 夫精神者所受於天也
fu jing shen zhe suo shou yu tian ye
It is the vital spirits that are received from heaven

42. 而形體者所稟於地也
er xing ti zhe suo lin yu di ye
And the body form that is provided by earth

43. 故曰
gu yue:
Thus it is said:

44. 一生二
yi sheng er
one gives rise to two

45. 二生三
er sheng san
two gives rise to three

46. 三 生 萬 物
san sheng wan wu
three gives rise to the ten thousand beings

47. 萬 物 背 陰 而 抱 陽
wan wu bei yin er bao yang
the ten thousand beings lean on the *yin* and embrace the *yang*

48. 沖 氣 以 為 和
chong qi yi wei he
and the powerful blending (*chong* 沖) of *qi* makes harmony (*he* 和)

Lines 44-48 are a direct quotation from Laozi chapter 42. This very well known chapter of the Laozi is frequently quoted as an illustration of Chinese cosmological thinking. However, it has often been translated in the past tense, whereas the Chinese concept of creation is one of constant change and renewal; it is not an event completed sometime in the distant past.

49. 故 曰
gu yue
Therefore it is said:

50. 一 月 而 膏
yi yue er gao
at one month it is a rich paste

> 'The first month is the beginning of taking a form, and by condensation and concentration there is the constitution of this fertile paste *gao* (膏) which is full of essences and life – full of the possibility of making an embryo.' (Pregnancy and Gestation; E. Rochat de la Vallée)

cf: Chunqiu Zuozhuan 10th year of Duke Cheng, which refers to vital substances symbolically located between diaphragm and heart, and states that disease could not be treated when it is in the *gao huang*, the intimate membranes of the body where life continually renews itself.

51. 二 月 而 胅
er yue er die
at two months it is a bulge

This suggests a swelling from within, as yeast swells; fire acting within water or *qi* acting on the vital essences.

52. 三 月 而 胎
san yue er tai
at three months it is a foetus

Three is the number associated with *qi,* and suggests the beginning of human form.

53. 四 月 而 肌
si yue er ji
at four months it has flesh

Four represents the possibility of taking form on earth. The flesh is the form of the body.

54. 五 月 而 筋
wu yue er jin
at five months it has sinews

The sinews allow development of muscular strength.

55. 六 月 而 骨
liu yue er gu
at six months it has bones

56. 七 月 而 成
qi yue er cheng
at seven months it is complete

57. 八 月 而 動
ba yue er dong
at eight months it moves

58. 九 月 而 躁
niu yue er zao
at nine months it quickens

59. 十 月 而 生
shi yue er sheng
at ten months it is born

Seven is the initial completion, but nine is the full achievement; it is born at ten.

This is one of the most ancient Chinese texts relating to embryology. It gives the essential numerology of the progression of human life, from coming into being (*sheng* 生) to completion (*cheng* 成). The number ten indicates completion and perfection, and according to the traditional interpretation of the scholars, this is seen in the character's combination of one single horizontal and one vertical stroke (十). Ten is also the number symbolically attributed to human beings: Ten months of gestation, and a life span of 10 x 10 = 100 years.

The first three months are attributed to the initial development and describe a gradual coherence; the three following months introduce the flesh, its movement and support; the three following months achieve internal organization and progressive autonomy of the foetus up to birth. This part of the text is discussed in detail in the Monkey Press book Pregnancy and Gestation. Similar descriptions are found in the Mawangdui texts, and are referred to in many later medical texts such as the Zhubing Yuanhou Lun and Sun Simiao.

60. 形 體 以 成
xing ti yi cheng
As the body form becomes complete

Here the text shows the formation and unfolding of human life according to the guidelines and principles of heaven. The body is seen as a manifestation of the cosmic order. Numerology is a way of describing these heavenly laws and the way in which they manifest on earth and within human beings.

61. 五 藏 乃 形
wu zang nai xing
The five organs then take form

The five organs (*wu zang* 五藏) are traditionally the heart, liver, spleen, lungs, kidneys within the system of *wu xing* (五 行), the five element correspondences. The five *zang* are the five elements within a human being. In Huainanzi chapter 7, the systemization of these correlations is not always the same as those found in other books, and lacks the more definitive classifications found in later medical texts. In line 65 the gallbladder is included amongst the *zang*, possibly alluding to its importance as the main decision-maker of the *zangfu* and its role as one of the extraordinary *fu*.

cf: The Extraordinary Fu, C. Larre and E. Rochat de la Vallée. Neijing Suwen chapter 11 sets down the definitive medical doctrine on *zang* and *fu* and extraordinary *fu*.

62. 是 故 肺 主 目
  shi gu fei zhu mu
  For this reason, the lungs master the eyes

63. 腎 主 鼻
  shen zhu bi
  The kidneys master the nose

64. 膽 主 口
  dan zhu kou
  The gallbladder masters the mouth

65. 肝 主 耳
  gan zhu er
  The liver masters the ears

As suggested above, these are not the correspondences found within the medical texts, but at this time in history there was not yet a systematic schemata of five element correspondences, such as is used in Chinese medicine up to the present time. The correspondences given here do not pertain to any medical texts that we know, though the attempt to show an inter-dependence between the internal organs and the sense organs remains the same.

66. 外 為 表
  wai wei biao
  The outer are for external expression

67. 而 內 為 裏
  er nei wei li
  And the internal are for inner organization

The *zang* (藏), internal organs, structure the innermost (*li* 裏), and the orifices and sense organs are their exterior (*biao* 表) manifestation in communication with the outside world. This is the same relationship between inside and outside seen in line 38, where the inside must rule the outside. Here the five *zang* must rule the sense organs.

68. 開 閉 張 歙
kai bi zhang xi
Opening and closing, expanding and contracting

Opening, *kai* (開), and closing, *bi* (閉), share the same radical, *men* (門), gate or door. *Kai* is a beginning, and *bi* its cessation. They continue the pairings of *biao li* (表 裏) and *nei wai* (內外) in lines 66 and 67, each expressing the fundamental rhythms of life at multiple levels.

69. 各 有 經 紀
ge you jing ji
Each has regulations and rules

Jing (經) is translated here as regulation, but is also the character translated in relation to acupuncture anatomy as meridian or channel. *Jing* (經) is also translated as a 'classic' text. Both describe the embodied influence of heaven, regulating and organizing the expression of life, both in the human body and in human society. (See note to line 8)

70. 故 頭 之 圓 也 象 天
gu tou zhi yuan ye xiang tian
Thus the roundness of the head is in the image of heaven

71. 足 之 方 也 象 地
zu zhi fang ye xiang di
The square made by the feet is in the image of earth

The image of heaven as a circle represents the cyclical passing of time, and the sequential movement of *qi* which makes the seasons and weather. The square of earth represents the space of the four quadrants (*si fang* 四方) on earth.

cf: Guanzi Neiye section 16:
'They will then be able to hold up the Great Circle (of the heavens)
And tread firmly over the Great Square (of the earth).' (H. D. Roth)

Also earlier in the Huainanzi, we see in chapter 3 section 2:
'The *dao* of heaven is called the circular, the *dao* of earth is called square.' (J. S. Major)

In this section of Huainanzi chapter 7, the image (*xiang* 象) of heaven and earth is given a bodily equivalence, following the passage in the text which details the formation of our human form. This is in contrast to the opening of the chapter, where before heaven and earth even existed, images were without form.

72. 天 有 四 時 五 行 九 解 三 百 六 十 六 日
tian you si shi wu xing jiu jie san bai liu shi liu ri
Heaven has four seasons, five moving forces, nine releasings and 366 days;

Here we have translated *wu xing* (五 行) as five moving forces, although it is more often translated as five phases, agents or elements. These are the natural regulation of the life process on earth, and when on earth, they are water, fire, wood, metal and earth. *Wu xing* is all of these things and more, and must always be understood in context. At this time in history, it was beginning to take on the meaning of the five specific manifestations of *qi*, related to five element cosmology. (cf: Wu Xing in Classical Chinese Texts, E. Rochat.) *Xing* also refers to the regular movement of the sun, moon and planets as seen in lines 86 and 90.

73. 人 亦 有 四 支 五 藏 九 竅 三 百 六 十 六 節
ren yi you si zhi wu zang jiu qiao san bai liu shi liu jie
human beings similarly have four limbs, five organs, nine orifices and 366 articulations.

The perfection of the human being 'made in the image of heaven' is shown through numerology (4 x 5 x 9 = 180 x 2 = 360). 366 is less anatomical than energetic, comprising 366 (or 360) relays or articulations. In the Lüshi Chunqui, (Annals of Lübuwei) 360 refers to the solar energy distributed through the days of the year, and in the same way energy circulates in the body by 360 relays (*jie* 節) of movement, or joints. The 366 joints may refer to all the small bone articulations of the body, but 366 is also the total number of acupuncture points on the body, as well as being an approximation of the days of the year. (cf: Lüshi Chunqiu XX 5)

The nine releasings *jie* (解) may allude to the nine levels of heaven, which are in both space and time. In line 72 they are linked with the nine apertures or orifices within the human body; here they probably refer to an opening in heaven, or from one level of heaven to another – hence the translation by releasings. This *jie* is to disentangle, to free up, to loosen.

In line 73, *jie* (節) suggests the articulations and joints of the body, as well as the knotting and binding along the pathways of the meridians. *Jie* (節) refers to the knots or stages of the growth of bamboo, which is reflected in the etymology of the character.

74. 天 有 風 雨 寒 暑
tian you feng yu han shu
Heaven has wind and rain, cold and heat;

75. 人 亦 有 取 與 喜 怒
ren yi you qu yu xi nu
human beings similarly have taking and giving, joy and anger.

Lines 74-75 make the direct analogy of meteorology with the inner climates of a human being. Joy and anger (*xi nu* 喜 怒) encompass all possible emotions and passions, as cold and heat represent all possible climates.

cf: Neijing Suwen chapter 5:
  'Heaven has four seasons and five elements
  For generating, growing, gathering and storing,
  And to produce cold, heat, dryness, dampness and wind.
  Man has five *zang* and, through transformation, five *qi,*
  Which produce joy, anger, sadness, grief and fear.'

76. 故 膽 為 雲
gu dan wei yun
Therefore the gallbladder makes clouds

77. 肺 為 氣
fei wei qi
the lungs *qi*

78. 肝 為 風
gan wei feng
the liver wind

79. 腎 為 雨
shen wei yu
the kidneys rain

80. 脾 為 雷
pi wei lei
the spleen thunder

Although this echoes the previous listing of the *zang*, here the spleen is also included.

cf: Neijing Suwen chapter 5:
> 'The *qi* of heaven communes with the lungs
> The *qi* of earth communes with the throat
> The *qi* of wind communes with the liver
> The *qi* of thunder communes with the heart
> The *qi* of the valleys communes with the spleen
> The *qi* of rain communes with the kidneys.'

81. 以 與 天 地 相 參 也 而 心 為 之 主
yi yu tian di xiang can ye er xin wei zhi zhu
There is mutual participation (*xiang can* 相 參) **with heaven and earth and the heart is master**

Human beings participate in the workings of heaven and earth and become one of the three powers. But they can only be a real partner with heaven and earth if the heart is enlightened by the spirits. This is the first time the heart (*xin* 心) is mentioned in the text and it is presented as a centre which naturally commands and rules. The heart as a centre is recognized within both Confucianism and Daoism.

The Huainanzi was written at the beginning of the Han Dynasty when China was firmly united around an emperor, and the establishment of the centre was seen as a natural necessity for the political life of the nation as well as for a human being. There is no natural order of life without the centre. The heart is seen as the centre of human life – a summation of all the five *zang*, and their natural leader *(zhu* 主*)*.

82. 是 故 耳 目 者 日 月 也
   shi gu er mu zhe ri yue ye
That is why ear and eye are sun and moon

83. 血 氣 者 風 雨 也
   xue qi zhe feng yu ye
Blood and qi are wind and rain

Human life and the human body are seen as a perfect reflection of the cosmic order.

84. 日 中 有 踆 烏
   ri zhong you cun wu
In the centre of the sun there is a three-legged crow

85. 而 月 中 有 蟾 蜍
   er yue zhong you chan chu
And in the middle of the moon there is a spotted toad

The toad and the crow are seen, for example, in the upper part of the Mawangdui funeral banner. *Cun wu* (踆烏) is the three-legged crow burnt jet black by the heat of the sun. Legend also tells us of a spotted toad, *chan chu (*蟾 蜍*)*, that lives in the moon. The toad eating the moon was seen as the agent of its waxing and waning. The crow and the toad have also become symbols for *yin* and *yang*. The crow is active during the day, flies in the sky and is therefore *yang* in nature; the toad is a creature of the night, and has an affinity with water, and is therefore *yin* in nature.

Upper part of the Mawangdui banner with black crow and spotted toad

86. 日 月 失 其 行
ri yue shi qi xing
When sun and moon lose their course (*xing* 行)

We have previously seen *xing* (行) in relation to the *wu xing* (五 行), or five phases and with the course of the five planets (see line 72). Here it is used to describe the ordered progression of the sun and moon.

87. 薄 蝕 無 光
bo shi wu guang
They catch and devour each other and there is no light

Solar and lunar eclipses are described in Chinese mythology as the sky wolf consuming its prey. Eclipses are very often a symbol of disaster. The sun and moon regulate and regenerate themselves, which symbolizes that all cycles naturally come to an end.

88. 風 雨 非 其 時
feng yu fei qi shi
When wind and rain are not in season

89. 毀 折 生 災
hui zhe sheng zai
They wreak havoc and bring about disaster

cf: Neijing Suwen chapter 2:
'When heaven retains its brilliant virtue, sun and moon are deprived of radiance … winds and rains are in disorder, the pearly dew does not descend…' (C. Larre, The Way of Heaven)

90. 五 星 失 其 行
wu xing shi qi xing
When the five planets lose their course

Note the homophones *xing* (星), planet and *xing* (行), orbiting circulation, or regulation. This again is the *xing* (行) of the *wu xing* (五行), five elements or phases, which represent nothing other than the celestial or natural order. The regularity or irregularity of heaven has a direct effect on earth and also on human beings and their stability.

91. 州 國 受 殃
zhou guo shou yang
The regions and states suffer catastrophe

92. 夫 天 地 之 道 至 紘 以 大
fu tian di zhi dao zhi hong yi da
The *dao* of heaven and earth by its ultimate immensity is great

93. 尚 猶 節 其 章 光 愛 其 神 明
shang you jie qi zhang guang ai qi shen ming

Yet it moderates its display of light and cares for the radiance of the spirits

Despite its immensity, the *dao* regulates the splendour of the universe in an orderly manner. *Guang* (光) light, refers to the *san guang*, (三光) the sun, moon and stars/planets. *Dao* (道) is the process, the way of life which is always in *yinyang* harmony, and which implies alternation, change and transformation. The rising and setting of the sun, day and night, is the model for activity and rest, and the moon waning and waxing a pattern for constant change. It is through alternation and transformation that life prospers. Sun and moon are the same as ears and eyes (see line 82). *Shen ming* (神 明) alludes to the splendour of the universe, which is the result of the natural development of the process of life in its correct rhythm (*jie* 節), translated here as to moderate. The radiance of heaven naturally illuminates human beings.

94. 人 之 耳 目 曷 能 久 熏 勞 而 不 息 乎
ren zhi er mu he neng jiu xun lao er bu xi hu

How can the ears and the eyes of man work long and hard without rest?

Ears and eyes refer to all the sense organs which are easily attracted by desires and must therefore be under the control of the heart and the spirits.

95. 精 神 何 能 久 馳 騁 而 不 既 乎
jing shen he neng jiu chi cheng er bu ji hu

How can the vital spirits race fast and furious without exhaustion?

Chi cheng (馳 騁) is the movement of two horses galloping wildly, and is a phrase commonly used for the desires and passions that disturb the heart.

cf: Laozi chapter 12:
'Racing and hunting (*chi cheng* 馳 騁) maddens the heart/mind (*xin* 心)'

96. 是 故 血 氣 者 人 之 華 也 而 五 藏 者 人 之 精 也
shi gu xue qi zhe ren zhi hua ye er wu zang zhe ren zhi jing ye

For this reason blood and *qi* are the splendour of man and the five organs are his essences

The splendour of blood and *qi* are visible at the exterior, arising from the inner vitality of the five organs. This is elaborated in medical texts, when the functioning of each organ is visible on the surface of the body through the blood and *qi,* in the skin, hair, nails, etc. These are referred to as the five splendours (*wu hua* 五華).

97. 夫 血 氣 能 專 於 五 藏 而 不 外 越
fu xue qi neng zhuan yu wu zang er bu wai yue

When blood and *qi* are concentrated in the five organs and not dispersed outside,

Blood and qi pervade the entire body but they are under the control of the five *zang* which integrate them and allow them to be beneficial to life.

98. 則 胸 腹 充 而 嗜 欲 省 矣
ze xiong fu chong er shi yu sheng yi

then chest and abdomen are replete, longing and desire diminish

Xiong fu (胸 腹), chest and abdomen, refers to the trunk of the body where the internal organs maintain life. When the organs are replete, or functioning fully, the blood and *qi* are rich and penetrating. This allows the body to be stable, which in turn encourages the presence of

the spirits. The presence of the spirits is a sign that we are aligned with
our true nature, and longings and desires naturally diminish.

99. 胸 腹 充 而 嗜 欲 省
　　xiong fu chong er shi yu sheng
**When chest and abdomen are replete, and longing and desires
diminished,**

100. 則 耳 目 清 聽 視 達 矣
　　ze er mu qing ting shi da yi
then ears and eyes are clear, hearing and seeing acute

The perceptions of the sense organs do not lead to longings and
desires which may disturb our view of things as they are.

101. 耳 目 清 聽 視 達
　　er mu qing ting shi da
When ears and eyes are clear, hearing and seeing acute

102. 謂 之 明
　　wei zhi ming
that is called illumination

When everything is functioning perfectly, the body is shining and
full of light, and the mind is clear. *Ming* (明) may be translated as
illumination, radiance, but also as enlightenment.

'Blood and *qi* make this inner illumination visible, but it is the five
zang which are the innermost essence of this expression of vitality.
The development and maintenance of the power of the *jing shen* (精
神), vital spirits, is fundamental. This clarity or illumination cannot

be disturbed by overuse of the sense organs or by the desires which cloud the mind, if they are ruled from a centre which is rooted in the nourishment of the *jing shen.'* (E. Rochat de la Vallée)

cf: Laozi chapter 3:
> 'Therefore the way the sage governs is to keep their hearts/minds empty and their bellies full.' (R. J. Lynn)

and Guanzi Neiye VIII:
> 'With a stable mind [heart, *xin* 心] at your core,
> With the eyes and ears acute and clear,
> And with the four limbs firm and fixed,
> You can thereby make a lodging place for the vital essence.'
> (H. D. Roth)

103. 五 藏 能 屬 於 心 而 無 乖
wu zang neng shu yu xin er wu guai
When the five organs are able to submit to the heart without resistance,

Shu yu (屬 於) is to depend on, to submit to, to be obedient to, and is the relationship of the five internal organs (*zang* 藏) to the heart. The heart cares for the other *zang,* and the *zang* depend on the heart in mutual relationship. This is not a forced submission, because the heart (emperor) embodies the consciousness of heaven. The organs are presented in this relationship of officials and sovereign in Neijing Suwen chapter 8, which is again symbolic of the natural order. (cf: The Secret Treatise of the Spiritual Orchid, Neijing Suwen chapter 8)

104. 則 教 志 勝 而 行 不 僻 矣
ze bo zhi sheng er xing bu pi yi
then however powerful the rising of the will, the behaviour does not deviate.

Perhaps also comparable to Confucius Analects II 4:
  'At seventy I could follow what my heart desired without
  transgressing what was right.' (J. Legge)

Also Suwen chapter 1 :
  'They restrained their will (*zhi* 志) and desire (*yu* 欲) diminished.
  At peace in their heart, they felt no fear. They worked hard
  and were not exhausted. The *qi* followed a regular course. Each
  followed his desire (*yu* 欲) and all were content.' (C. Larre)

105. 敦 志 勝 而 行 之 不 僻
        bo zhi sheng er xing zhi bu pi
**However powerful the rising of the will, if the behaviour does not
deviate,**

106. 則 精 神 盛 而 氣 不 散 矣
        ze jing shen sheng er qi bu san yi
then the vital spirits thrive and the *qi* are not scattered.

107. 精 神 盛 而 氣 不 散 則 理
        jing shen sheng er qi bu san ze li
**When the vital spirits thrive and the *qi* are not scattered, then
there is perfect order.**

Li (理) suggests the innate order or principle which reflects a natural
or heavenly organization. The etymology of the character alludes to the
veins in a piece of jade, which reveal the inner life within its structure.
It is the visible aspect of the natural order and its underlying meaning.

108. 理 則 均
        li ze jun
perfect order, then equilibrium

Jun (均) is equilibrium, equality in a dynamic situation, inner balance.
Equilibrium arises through the innate ability to find balance.

109. 均 則 通
jun ze tong
equilibrium, then free communication

Tong (通) implies a complete penetration or permeation; to commune
with, an all pervasive intermingling. It is also to perceive, to know
thoroughly, to understand perfectly. Neijing Suwen Chapter 3 is
entitled '*sheng qi tong tian lun*' (生 氣 通 天 論) 'The *qi* of living
beings communes with heaven'. *Tong* is frequently used in medicine to
describe the healthy permeation and circulation of *qi*.

110. 通 則 神
tong ze shen
free communication, then the spirits

When everything in the body and mind is flowing and communicating
well, the spirits are present. With the vital spirits flourishing, everything
returns to the natural organization of life (*li* 理).

111. 神 則
shen ze
With the spirits

112. 以 視 無 不 見
yi shi wu bu jian
in looking there is nothing that is not seen

113. 以 聽 無 不 聞 也
yi ting wu bu wen ye
in listening there is nothing that is not heard

114. 以 為 無 不 成 也
yi wei wu bu cheng ye
in doing there is nothing that is not accomplished

The virtues arising from the presence of the spirits are presented through a series of double negatives (*wu bu* 無 不). These involve the senses of sight, hearing and action, so that even the invisible is seen, and in doing there is nothing that is not accomplished, because it is done in harmony with the natural process of life.

115. 是 故 憂 患 不 能 入 也 而 邪 氣 不 能 襲
shi gu you huan bu neng ru ye er xie qi bu neng xi
Thus worries and concerns cannot enter and perverse *qi* cannot strike

The basis of the practice of authentic traditional medicine is to nourish the *jing shen* as the way of regulating and strengthening the inner unity, and hence immunity, so that invaders cannot enter, even by surprise attack. The five *zang* which are the basis of all vital functions, cannot work well unless they are inspired by the spirits. This allows them to act according to their true nature and the natural order.

116. 故 事 有 求 之 於 四 海 之 外 而 不 能 遇
gu shi you qiu zhi yu si hai zhi wai er bu neng yu
Though actively seeking it beyond the four seas it cannot be found

The term 'four seas' describes the unknown extremities of the four directions, and suggests something that is beyond the limit of our comprehension.

117. 或 守 之 於 形 骸 之 內 而 不 見 也
huo shou zhi yu xing hai zhi nei er bu jian ye
And guarding it within the physical form it cannot be seen

Xing hai (形 骸) is the physical form, *hai* referring to the bony structure. This is objective existence, the human body itself.

118. 故 所 求 多 者 所 得 少
gu suo qiu duo zhe suo de shao
Therefore, those who seek too much gain less

119. 所 見 大 者 所 知 小
suo jian da zhe suo zhi xiao
Those who look for the great know little

Laozi chapter 47:

'Without going out of your door you can know the ways of the world. Without peeping through your window you can see the way of heaven. The farther you go, the less you know. Thus the sage knows without travelling, sees without looking and achieves without ado.' (J. C. Wu)

120. 夫 孔 竅 者 精 神 之 戶 牖 也
fu kong qiao zhe jing shen zhi hu you ye
Openings and orifices are the windows and doors of the vital spirits

The vital spirits, *jing shen,* give the ability to see clearly and hear with fidelity. To function well the orifices need the presence of the vital spirits.

121. 而 氣 志 者 五 藏 之 使 候 也
er qi zhi zhe wu zang zhi shi hou ye

And *qi* and will are the messengers and stewards of the five organs

The steward wears the special livery of the house of the master and introduces only those whom the master wants to see. Both messengers and stewards carry out the instructions of the master.

122. 耳 目 淫 於 聲 色 之 樂
er mu yin yu sheng se zhi le

When ears and eyes are corrupted by the pleasures of sounds and colours,

cf: Laozi chapter 12:
'The five colours blind the eye
The five tones deafen the ear' (J. C. Wu)

'If the five internal organs are unable to regulate the sense organs, then they are disturbed by desires which enter through the sense organs. This is as if a steward were to allow thieves into the house. Then the five internal organs are no longer in touch with their spiritual foundation, and are less able to send correct messengers and messages. If the organ is overcome by desire and passion, the movement of *qi* is disorganized. In medicine, this is the basis of the pathology of the "wills of the five organs" which are unable to control blood and *qi* correctly.' (E. Rochat de la Vallée)

cf: Neijing Suwen chapter 5:
'...anger injures the liver
...elation injures the heart
...obsessive thought injures the spleen
...oppressive grief injures the lungs
...fear injures the kidneys'

123. 則 五 藏 搖 動 而 不 定 矣
ze wu zang yao dong er bu ding yi
then the five organs are shaken and rattled and have no stability

124. 五 藏 搖 動 而 不 定
wu zang yao dong er bu ding
When the five organs, shaken and rattled, have no stability,

125. 則 血 氣 滔 蕩 而 不 休 矣
ze xue qi tao dang er bu xiu yi
then blood and *qi* overflow recklessly and do not settle

126. 血 氣 滔 蕩 而 不 休
xue qi tao dang er bu xiu
When the blood and *qi* overflow recklessly and do not settle,

127. 則 精 神 馳 騁 於 外 而 不 守 矣
ze jing shen chi cheng yu wai er bu shou yi
**then the vital spirits race fast and furious out of bounds and are
not contained**

If mental capacity is used against the innate nature and the heart
becomes prey to desires and passions, then one lives for the fulfilment
of desire and not for the fulfilment of destiny.

128. 精 神 馳 騁 於 外 而 不 守
jing shen chi cheng yu wai er bu shou
**When the vital spirits race fast and furious out of bounds and are
not contained,**

cf: Neijing Lingshu chapter 8, which describes a situation where blood and *qi* are in disorder and the *shen* can no longer remain in the internal organs *(zang)*. There is uncontrollable agitation, confusion and disorder. (The Heart in Lingshu chapter 8)

129. 則 禍 福 之 至 雖 如 丘 山 無 由 識 之 矣
ze huo fu zhi zhi sui ru qiu shan wu you shi zhi yi
then even if good or bad fortune were as imposing as a mountain, there would be no way of recognizing them for what they are

Intelligence and clarity of mind come from the presence of the spirits and the communication of the spirits with heaven. The development of spiritual power at a human level may imply skilfulness and artfulness, but not necessarily a true vision of reality.

130. 使 耳 目 精 明 玄 達 而 無 誘 慕
shi er mu jing ming xuan da er wu you mu
If ear and eye are clear and bright, deep and penetrating, and do not yearn or covet;

131. 氣 志 虛 靜 恬 愉 而 省 嗜 欲
qi zhi xu jing tian yu er sheng shi yu
if *qi* and will are empty and serene, calm and content, and longings and desires diminish;

132. 五 藏 定 寧 充 盈 而 不 泄
wu zang ding ning chong ying er bu xie
if the five organs are stable and tranquil, satisfied and replete, and nothing leaks away;

133. 精 神 內 守 形 骸 而 不 外 越
   jing shen nei shou xing hai er bu wai yue
if the vital spirits are contained within the physical form, and are not dispersed outside –

cf: Guanzi Neiye XIII:
   'Then the eyes and ears won't overflow
   And the mind [heart] will have nothing else to seek' (H. D. Roth)

cf: Neijing Suwen chapter 44
   'If obsessive thoughts (*si* 思) carry on indefinitely, and one does not succeed in getting what one aspires to, then the intent (*yi* 意) is scattered uncontrollably on the outside (*wai* 外).'

134. 則 望 於 往 世 之 前 而 視 於 來 事 之 後
   ze wang yu wang shi zhi qian er shi yu lai shi zhi hou
then the vision extends beyond what came before the past and reaches to what is after the future

When the vital spirits see with vision, they naturally perceive that which is beyond time and space.
cf: Xici:
   'What *yin yang* cannot fathom, that is the spirits.'

135. 猶 未 足 為 也
   you wei zu wei ye
Even that is not enough!

136. 豈 直 禍 福 之 間 哉
   qi zhi huo fu zhi jian zai
So how is it possible to distinguish between good and bad fortune?

137. 故 曰 其 出 彌 遠 者 其 知 彌 少
gu yue qi chu mi yuan zhe qi zhi mi shao
It is said: 'the further one goes the less one knows'

cf: Laozi chapter 47, referred to in note to line 119

138. 以 言 夫 精 神 之 不 可 使 外 淫 也
yi yan fu jing shen zhi bu ke shi wai yin ye
This means that one should not allow the vital spirits to move outward and degenerate

139. 是 故 五 色 亂 目　 使 目 不 明
shi gu wu se luan mu shi mu bu ming
So, when the five colours confuse the eye, the eye cannot see clearly.

140. 五 聲 譁 耳 使 耳 不 聰
wu sheng hua er shi er bu cong
When the five sounds deafen the ear, the ear cannot hear acutely.

141. 五 味 亂 口 使 口 爽 傷
wu wei luan kou shi kou shuang shang
When the five tastes confuse the mouth, the palate is spoiled.

cf: Laozi chapter 12 referred to in note to line 122.
Also Zhuangzi chapter 12.

142. 趣 舍 滑 心 使 行 飛 揚
qu she gu xin shi xing fei yang
When attractions and aversions trouble the heart, actions fly astray.

143. 此 四 者 天 下 之 所 養 性 也 然 皆 人 累 也
ci si zhe tian xia zhi suo yang xing ye ran jie ren lei ye

By these four, all under heaven nourish their innate nature, only human beings become bound.

Only human beings become bound up in desires and longings, get tied up in knots and are no longer able to embody the vital spirits.

144. 故 曰 嗜 欲 者 使 人 之 氣 越
gu yue shi yu zhe shi ren zhi qi yue

So it is said: longing and desire cause the *qi* of man to be dispersed,

145. 而 好 憎 者 使 人 之 心 勞
er hao zeng zhe shi ren zhi xin lao

and liking and loathing cause the heart of man to be weary.

146. 弗 疾 去 則 志 氣 日 耗
fu ji qu ze zhi qi ri hao

If they are not immediately expelled, then will and *qi* deteriorate day by day.

'*Qi* and will' represent all the inner movements of life which are controlled by the heart and transmitted to the five internal organs. The will is easily led astray by desire – by what I want and what I reject.

147. 夫 人 之 所 以 不 能 終 其 壽 命
fu ren zhi suo yi bu neng zhong qi shou ming

Why are men unable to reach the end of their given lifespan

148. 而 中 道 夭 於 刑 戮 者 何 也
er zhong dao yao yu xing lu zhe he ye
but die young midway, through punishment or execution?

This is a common query and is, for example, the opening question of the Yellow Emperor to his physician in the art of medicine in Neijing Suwen chapter 1:

> ' Nowadays humans, halfway to their 100 years, all decline in activity.' (C. Larre, The Way of Heaven)

149. 以 其 生 生 之 厚
yi qi sheng sheng zhi hou
It is because they live their life too fully.

Hou (厚), generous, substantial, here suggests living life to excess. A life controlled by desire is by definition never to have enough – to be insatiable – therefore we are never content. Not to have enough is a sign of losing the way.

cf: Laozi chapter 44:
> 'If you know when to stop, you'll suffer no harm.
> And in this way you can last a very long time. (R. G. Hendricks)

cf: Laozi chapter 50:
> 'We emerge into life, enter into death. Three out of ten are adherents of life; three out of ten are adherents of death; and there are three out of ten whose way of life also leads them to death. Why is this so? It is due to placing too much emphasis on life.' (R. D. Lynn)

150. 夫 惟 能 無 以 生 為 者 則 所 以 脩 得 生 也
fu wei neng wu yi sheng wei zhe ze suo yi xiu de sheng ye
Only those who do not live for life obtain long life.

Life is a temporary union of heaven and earth, so will not last. Long life is not not to die – but not to restrict life to what happens between birth and death.

cf: Lüshi Chunqiu III, 2
'… The vital essence and the spirit being secure within the bodily frame, the person's life span is extended. This extension is not a matter of lengthening a short life, but of fulfilling an allotted span.' (J. Knoblock & J. Riegel)

151. 夫 天 地 運 而 相 通
fu tian di yun er xiang tong
So heaven and earth revolve in mutual exchange,

Yun 運 is the revolving or rotating movement of heaven and earth. The phrase 'yun er xiang tong' (運 而 相 通), means mutually penetrating or engaging together in the distribution of influences. *Tian yun* (天 運) refers to the regular movement of the stars and planets, as well as the distribution and mutual exchange of influences of these celestial bodies, as they revolve one with another. *Xiang tong* suggests mutual penetration, as in making love, where it is both a physical and spiritual co-penetration. Here it is the communing of heaven and earth.

152. 萬 物 總 而 為 一
wan wu zong er wei yi
and the ten thousand beings altogether make the One.

The ten thousand beings are the result of this constant interchange of heaven and earth and constitute the One. They are the myriad expressions of life which manifest themselves with various forms and appearances, but which maintain the same core of reality. All things proceed from the *dao* and remain in the process of life – this is called Oneness, the unity.

153. 能 知 一 則 無 一 之 不 知 也
neng zhi yi ze wu yi zhi bu zhi yi
For those able to know the One – not one thing is unknown.

If understanding is not based in this vision of the One, it will always be partial – both incomplete and biased.

154. 不 能 知 一 　 則 無 一 之 能 知 也
bu neng zhi yi 　 ze wu yi zhi neng zhi ye
For those unable to know the One – nothing can be known.

155. 譬 吾 處 於 天 下 也
pi wu chu yu tian xia ye
If we consider our place in the world,

Tian xia (天下) can be translated as all under heaven, the world, the empire according to context.

156. 亦 為 一 物 矣
yi wei yi wu yi
it is the place of one being.

Each of us is just one amongst the myriad of beings.

157. 不 識 天 下 之 以 我 備 其 物 與
bu shi tian xia zhi yi wo bei qi wu yu
I do not know whether the world completes its collection of beings through me,

158. 且 惟 無 我 而 物 無 不 備 者 乎
qie wei wu wo er wu wu bu bei zhe hu
**or whether its collection of beings would still be complete without
me.**

How can I know if I am a necessary or significant part of the whole?
Without me the whole will still be the whole: nothing can increase or
decrease the *dao.* But if I do exist, I have to participate in the whole in
order to make it the whole. And for a human being that participation is
to become like a spirit of heaven; to cultivate oneself to become as *jing
shen.*

159. 然 則 我 亦 物 也
ran ze wo yi wu ye
Indeed I am also a being.

160. 物 亦 物 也
wu yi wu ye
A being amongst beings.

161. 物 之 與 物 也
wu zhi yu wu ye
Beings in relation to other beings.

162. 又 何 以 相 物 也
you he yi xiang wu ye
How can beings be distinguished from one another?

If we take it that everything is a being, how can they be differentiated?
And what is the point of making the distinction? Is it more important
to be an individual or part of the whole, integrated into the unity of
the cosmos? *Xiang* (相) suggests a reciprocity, as well as the ability

to distinguish. It is, however, also the term used for the practice of physiognomy, which is the observation of external appearance in order to understand an individual's true nature (*xing* 性) and destiny (*ming* 命).

Huainanzi chapter 7 begins with the immensity of heaven and earth; lines 155-169 move the enquiry to the level of individual beings in the world, and asks what distinguishes us in our relationships one with another. If we are all the same, how can we differentiate each other and what is the status of the individual?

163. 雖 然
sui ran
Even so

164. 其 生 我 也 將 以 何 益
qi sheng wo ye jiang yi he yi
What gain is there for giving me life?

165. 其 殺 我 也 將 以 何 損
qi sha wo ye jiang yi he sun
What loss for taking my life away?

166. 夫 造 化 者 既 以 我 為 坯 矣
fu zao hua zhe ji yi wo wei pi yi
That which produces and transforms moulds me like clay

167. 將 無 所 違 之 矣
jiang wu suo wei zhi yi
I would have no reason to resist

168. 吾 安 知 夫 刺 灸 而 欲 生 者 之 非 惑 也
wu an zhi fu ci jiu er yu sheng zhe zhi fei huo ye
How can we know if the one who has needles and moxa in the desire to live, is not deluded?

169. 又 安 知 夫 絞 經 而 求 死 者 之 非 福 也
you an zhi fu jiao jing er qiu si zhe zhi fei fu ye
How can we know if one who ties a cord around his neck seeking death, is not fortunate?

170. 或 者 生 乃 徭 役 也
huo zhe sheng nai yao yi ye
Perhaps life is just forced labour

171. 而 死 乃 休 息 也
er si nai xiu xi ye
and death just rest

cf: Zhuangzi chapter 2:
'How do I know that loving life is not a delusion? How do I know that in hating death I am not like a man who having left home in his youth, has forgotten the way back.' (B. Watson)

and Liezi chapter 7, where life is described as hard work, death as rest.

172. 天 下 茫 茫 孰 知 之 哉
tian xia mang mang shu zhi zhi zai
The world is vast and wide – how can it be known?

173. 其 生 我 也 不 彊 求 已
qi sheng wo ye bu qiang qiu yi
Life is given to me – I do not try to end it

174. 其 殺 我 也 不 彊 求 止
qi sha wo ye bu qiang qiu zhi
Life is taken from me – I do not try to stop it

175. 欲 生 而 不 事
yu sheng er bu shi
I desire life – but make nothing of it

176. 憎 死 而 不 辭
zeng si er bu ci
I loathe death – but do not refuse it

177. 賤 之 而 弗 憎
jian zhi er fu zeng
Being lowly – I do not loathe it

178. 貴 之 而 弗 喜
gui zhi er fu xi
Being noble – I do not rejoice in it

179. 隨 其 天 資 而 安 之 不 極
sui qi tian zi er an zhi bu ji
I follow the disposition of heaven and content in this, do not push beyond

180. 吾 生 也 有 七 尺 之 形
wu sheng ye you qi chi zhi xing
In life we have a body of seven feet

181. 吾 死 也 有 一 棺 之 土
wu si ye you yi guan zhi tu
In death we occupy one coffin in the earth

182. 吾 生 之 比 於 有 形 之 類
wu sheng zhi bi yu you xing zhi lei
In life we belong to the category of what has form

183. 猶 吾 死 之 淪 於 無 形 之 中 也
you wu si zhi lun yu wu xing zhi zhong ye
In death we are engulfed in the midst of the formless

184. 然 則 吾 生 也 物 不 以 益 眾
ran ze wu sheng ye wu bu yi yi zhong
So, alive we do not increase the multitude of beings

185. 吾 死 也 土 不 以 加 厚
wu si ye tu bu yi jia hou
Dead, we do not add to the thickness of the earth

186. 吾 又 安 知 所 喜 憎 利 害 其 間 者 乎
wu you an zhi suo xi zeng li hai qi jian zhe hu
How could I know the difference between joy and loathing, benefit and harm?

187. 夫 造 化 者 之 攫 援 物 也 譬 猶 陶 人 之 埏 埴 也
fu zao hua zhe zhi jue yuan wu ye pi you tao ren zhi shan zhi ye

Now, that which produces and transforms takes hold of a being as a potter works clay.

Zao hua (造 化) is a common way to speak of the process of the *dao* in its production and transformation of life.

188. 其 取 之 地 而 已 為 盆 盎 也
qi qu zhi di er yi wei pen ang ye

The clay taken from the earth and shaped into a bowl or dish

189. 與 其 未 離 於 地 也 無 以 異
yu qi wei li yu di ye wu yi yi

is no different from the clay which is not yet separated from the earth.

190. 其 已 成 器 而 破 碎 漫 瀾 而 復 歸 其 故 也
qi yi cheng qi er po sui man lan er fu gui qi gu ye

Having become a utensil it will be shattered into small pieces, dispersed and dissolved and return to its former state.

A potter takes a handful of clay from the unformed mass in the earth and gives it form. By taking form, a utensil comes into being and according to its specific attributes this utensil will have a specific use. When it is broken, the pieces of the pot will merge again into the mass of clay in the potter's field.

191. 與 其 為 盆 盎 亦 無 以 異 矣
yu qi wei pen ang yi wu yi yi yi

Compared to when it was a bowl or dish, there is no difference.

The reality of our life remains the same – before birth and after death. It comes into form and returns to the formless. If we become attached to the form (the bowl) we forget the potentiality of the vital spirits.

192. 夫 臨 江 之 鄉 居 人 汲 水 以 浸 其 園 江 水 弗 憎 也

fu lin jiang zhi xiang ju ren ji shui yi jin qi yuan jiang shui fu zeng ye

Now, in the villages by the river, they draw water to soak their gardens; the water from the river feels no resentment.

193. 苦 洿 之 家 決 洿 而 注 之 江 洿 水 弗 樂 也

ku wu zhi jia jue wu er zhu zhi jiang wu shui fu le ye

Families plagued by stagnant water open a passage for it to flow into the river; the stagnant water feels no pleasure.

194. 是 故 其 在 江 也 無 以 異 其 浸 園 也

shi gu qi zai jiang ye wu yi yi qi jin yuan ye

This is because the water in the river is no different from the water soaking the gardens.

195. 其 在 洿 也 亦 無 以 異 其 在 江 也

qi zai wu ye yi wu yi yi qi zai jiang ye

In the same way the stagnant water is no different from the water in the river.

196. 是 故 聖 人 因 時 以 安 其 位

shi gu sheng ren yin shi yi an qi wei

Therefore the sage:

Following the appropriate time is content in his position

cf: Zhuangzi chapter 6:
'He is chilly like autumn, balmy like spring, and his joy and anger prevail throughout the four seasons.' (B. Watson)

197. 當 世 而 樂 其 業
dang shi er le qi ye
Adapting to the age takes pleasure in his activities

This line refers to the circumstances in human society.

198. 夫 悲 樂 者 德 之 邪 也
fu bei le zhe de zhi xie ye
Sadness and happiness are perversions of the *de*

De (德) is the revelation of the *dao*, the *dao* manifesting itself. As such it is the vital force of an individual, dependent on individual nature and behaviour. The more individuals are attuned to the heavenly order, the more their ability (power) to accomplish a particular action.

199. 而 喜 怒 者 道 之 過 也
er xi nu zhe dao zhi guo ye
And joy and anger are deviations from the *dao*

Joy and happiness may reflect an unbalanced emotion within the Chinese understanding, causing disturbance to the natural contentment and stillness of the heart.

200. 好 憎 者 心 之 暴 也
hao zeng zhe xin zhi bao ye
Likes and dislikes do violence to the heart

201. 故 曰
gu yue
Therefore it is said:

202. 其 生 也 天 行
qi sheng ye tian xing
'His life is a movement of heaven

203. 其 死 也 物 化
qi si ye wu hua
His death a transformation of things

204. 靜 則 與 陰 俱 閉
jing ze yu yin ju bi
In stillness he shares the closing of the *yin*

205. 動 則 與 陽 俱 開
dong ze yu yang ju kai
In motion he shares the opening of the *yang'*

cf: Zhuangzi chapter 13:
    'Hence it is said: 'Whoever knows the joy from Heaven
    In his life proceeds with Heaven,
    In his death transforms with other things,
    In stillness shares the Power in the Yin,
    In motion shares the surge of the Yang.' (A. C. Graham)

'The sage is one with the process of life, with the way of heaven. Having no will or desire he follows the movement of cosmic life. He comes into life when heaven or nature makes him appear, and disappears when it is time to continue another kind of life through transformation. Not acting by his own volition, he follows the *yin* and the *yang*, for example in the seasons or in any moment or circumstance.' (E. Rochat de la Vallée)

206. 精 神 澹 然 無 極
jing shen dan ran wu ji
His vital spirits being calm, are without limit

cf: Zhuangzi chapter 13:
> 'The sage is not still because he takes stillness to be good and therefore is still. The ten thousand things are insufficient to distract his mind (heart) – that is the reason he is still.' (B. Watson)

The serenity of the *jing shen* comes from the perfect alternation of *yin yang*. In this serenity nothing is out of balance. There is limitless (*wu ji* 無 極) calm.

207. 不 與 物 散
bu yu wu san
He does not let himself be dissipated by beings

208. 而 天 下 自 服
er tian xia zi fu
And all under heaven naturally yield to him

209. 故 心 者 形 之 主 也
gu xin zhe xing zhi zhu ye
Thus the heart is master of the body,

210. 而 神 者 心 之 寶 也
er shen zhe xin zhi bao ye
and spirits the treasure of the heart.

211. 形 勞 而 不 休 則 蹶 精 用 而 不 已 則 竭
xing lao er bu xiu ze jue jing yong er bu yi ze jie
The body labouring without rest collapses, essences used unceasingly run dry.

212. 是 故 聖 人 貴 而 尊 之 不 敢 越 也
shi gu sheng ren gui er zun zhi bu gan yue ye
Therefore the sage appreciates and values them, and does not dare abuse them.

213. 夫 有 夏 后 氏 之 璜 者 匣 匱 而 藏 之 寶 之 至 也
fu you xia hou shi zhi huang zhe xia kui er cang zhi bao zhi zhi ye
The semicircular jade of Xia Hou is stored in a secure box because it is a treasure of the utmost value.

The *huang*, or semi-circular jade, was an ancient ritual object. The smaller jades were worn on the body as protection, the larger used for ceremonial purposes within the temple or household. They invoked the protection of the deity of the North. Xia Hou is an ancient title for the legendary emperor Yu the Great.

214. 夫 精 神 之 可 寶 也 非 直 夏 后 氏 之 璜 也
fu jing shen zhi ke bao ye fei zhi xia hou shi zhi huang ye

Now, are not the essences and spirits more precious than the semicircular jade of Xia Hou?

In Chinese medicine, essences and spirits (the vital spirits) are two of the *san bao* (三 寶) or 'three treasures' – *jing, qi, shen*.

cf: Zhuangzi chapter 15:
> The man who owns a sword from Gan or Yue lays it in a box and stores it away, not daring to use it, for to him it is the greatest of treasures. ...The way to purity and whiteness is to guard the spirit (*shen* 神), this alone; guard it and never lose it, and you will become one with spirit, one with its pure essence (*jing* 精)...
> (Based on the translation by B. Watson)

215. 是 故 聖 人 以 無 應 有 必 究 其 理
shi gu sheng ren yi wu ying you bi jiu qi li

Therefore the sage responds to what is by means of what is not and so penetrates its inner principle (*li* 理).

Wu (無) is that which does not exist, that which is without form or features, the state before manifestation. *You* (有) is that which exists, has form and determination. *Li* (理) is here translated as inner principle (see note to line 107).

cf: Laozi chapter 11:
> Therefore, we regard having something (*you* 有) as beneficial;
> But having nothing (*wu* 無) as useful.' (R. G. Hendricks)

Laozi chapter 40:
> 'The things of the world originate in being (*you* 有),
> And being originates in nonbeing (*wu* 無).' (R. G. Hendricks)

216. 以 虛 受 實 必 窮 其 節
yi xu shou shi bi qiong qi jie

By means of emptiness he receives its fullness and so fathoms its rhythms.

Both *jie* (節) (see note line 73) and *li* (理) (see note 107) suggest the inner reality of life, its integral rhythms and structuration. Once this is perceived, one can negotiate physical reality without strain.

217. 恬 愉 虛 靜 以 終 其 命
tian yu xu jing yi zhong qi ming

Calm and content, empty and still, he fulfils his destiny.

Ming (命) is the mandate of heaven within a human being, the allotted lifespan and life purpose.

218. 是 故 無 所 甚 疏 而 無 所 甚 親
shi gu wu suo shen shu er wu suo shen qin

Therefore, nothing is very distant from him and nothing is very close.

The usual limits of time and space no longer apply to him.

219. 抱 德 煬 和 以 順 于 天
bao de yang he yi shun yu tian

Embracing the *de*, merging harmoniously, he follows heaven.

(See line 198 on *de* (德))

220. 與 道 為 際 與 德 為 鄰
yu dao wei ji yu de wei lin

Side by side with the *dao*, neighbours with the *de*,

221. 不 為 福 始 不 為 禍 先
bu wei fu shi bu wei he xian

he does not make good fortune his premise nor bad fortune his precedent.

Because good and bad fortune are mundane values.

222. 魂 魄 處 其 宅 而 精 神 守 其 根
hun po chu qi zhai er jing shen shou qi gen

***Hun* and *po* keep their places and the vital spirits guard his root.**

Hun (魂) and *po* (魄) are two aspects of the soul within a human being. The *hun* are related to the intangible, the mind and spirit, and will return to heaven at death. The *po* are attached to the body and will return to the earth.

223. 死 生 無 變 於 己 故 曰 至 神
si sheng wu bian yu ji gu yue zhi shen

For him death and life are not a change, therefore he is called a perfect spirit.

Death and life are not a change because he is already in a state of mind beyond them. His mind and consciousness have merged with what is before life and after death.

224. 所 謂 真 人 者 性 合 于 道 也
suo wei zhen ren zhe xing he yu dao ye

To be called an authentic man means that his nature is united with the *dao*.

cf: Neijing Suwen chapter 1:
    'There were authentic men who had grasped heaven and earth

Held *yin yang* in their hands
And breathed with the essences and *qi* [pure, subtle and vital *qi, jing qi*]
Established in themselves by keeping the spirits
In their flesh they realized the Oneness'

225. 故 有 而 若 無
gu you er ruo wu
Therefore, being is the same as not being

Being and not being, what is and what is not, are translations of *you* and *wu*. (See note to line 215) *You* literally means to have and to be, and in its opposition to *wu*, suggests that which has form and volition, as opposed to that which has none, but contains all potential. In philosophical texts, they may refer to the presence or absence of perceptible qualities, but also to the presence or absence of deliberation or conscious effort.

226. 實 而 若 虛
shi er ruo xu
Fullness is the same as emptiness

cf: Laozi chapter 4
  'The Tao is like an empty bowl,
   Which in being used can never be filled up.' (J. C. Wu)

227. 處 其 一 不 知 其 二
chu qi yi bu zhi qi er
Dwelling in oneness he does not know the two

'Being in oneness is to abandon any discursive thinking, any analysis, any conscious awareness. One cannot be in oneness and at the same time be aware of being in oneness.' (E. Rochat de la Vallée)

228. 治 其 內 不 識 其 外
zhi qi nei bu shi qi wai
Absorbed in the interior he pays no attention to the exterior

(see note to line 38)

229. 明 白 太 素 無 為 復 樸
ming bai tai su wu wei fu pu
In pure illumination, great simplicity and non-doing, he returns to the uncarved block

Pu (樸) the un-carved block, is used as a metaphor for primal simplicity, original nature, undifferentiated being. The wood from a tree is full of potential, it is untreated and uncarved by human hand. Once it has been carved into a specific form, it no longer contains all the possibilities implicit in wholeness.

cf: Laozi chapters 15 and 28

230. 體 本 抱 神
ti ben bao shen
He embodies the origin and embraces spirit

The origin is the root, the source; it is by returning to the root that one can return to one's true nature and unite with the *dao*. Free from the bonds of individual form and characteristics, one's vital spirits may roam in the immensity of the universe.

231. 以 游 于 天 地 之 樊 芒 然 彷 徉 于 塵 垢 之 外
yi you yu tian di zhi fan mang ran pang yang yu chen gou zhi wai

而 消 搖 于 無 事 之 業
er xiao yao yu wu shi zhi ye

Roaming in the enclosure of heaven and earth, wandering obliviously to and fro beyond the dusty world, and ambling about occupied with non-activity.

232. 浩 浩 蕩 蕩 乎
hao hao dang dang hu
Vast! Boundless!

233. 機 械 知 巧 弗 載 於 心
ji xie zhi qiao fu zai yu xin
Cleverness and skilfulness do not burden his heart.

Someone relying on skilfulness and cleverness is always limited by them. For the sage, the accurate answer to any question will come immediately from within.

cf: Laozi chapter 48:
'The pursuit of learning is to increase day after day.
The pursuit of Tao is to decrease day after day.'
(Wing-tsit Chan)

234. 是 故 死 生 亦 大 矣 而 不 為 變
shi gu si sheng yi da yi er bu wei bian
Therefore death and life are of equal importance and neither is a change.

235. 雖 天 地 覆 育 亦 不 與 之 抮 抱 矣

sui tian di fu yu yi bu yu zhi zhen bao yi

Although heaven covers him and earth nurtures him, he does not cling to them.

236. 審 乎 無 瑕 而 不 與 物 糅

shen hu wu xia er bu yu `wu rou

He scrutinizes the flawless and does not get mixed up with things.

237. 見 事 之 亂 而 能 守 其 宗

jian shi zhi luan er neng shou qi zong

Perceiving the confusion of worldly affairs he is still able to preserve his ancestral origin.

Zong (宗) suggests the origination of an ancestral or dynastic line. In medicine the *zong qi* (宗 氣) is the personal, usable *qi*, and also suggests the ability to identify that which is authentically part of oneself.

238. 若 然 者 忘 肝 膽 遺 耳 目

ruo ran zhe wang gan dan yi er mu

Men like that forget their liver and gall, neglect their ears and eyes,

This is to forget both the inner and outer life. Here we have assumed an error in the use of the character *zheng* (正) and have substituted *wang* (忘), to forget.

239. 心 志 專 于 內 通 達 耦 于 一

xin zhi zhuan yu nei tong da ou yu yi

and with their heart and will concentrated within, their penetration and comprehension make them companions with the One.

'The two characters heart (*xin* 心) and will (*zhi* 志) used together, suggest the whole functioning of the mind, with its determination, resoluteness, strength of character and purposefulness – as when one puts one's heart and soul into something. When this concentration is turned within, to the depths of one's heart, one finds the heart of the universe, the spirits of heaven, the source of life.' (E. Rochat de la Vallée)

240. 居 不 知 所 為 行 不 知 所 之 渾 然 而 往 逯 然 而 來
    ju bu zhi suo wei xing bu zhi suo zhi hun ran er wang lu ran er lai

Staying still, they do not know what they are doing, on the move they do not know where they are going; chaotically they go and randomly they come.

Here 'chaotic' is to be beyond the distinction of form. Chaos is not a negative but the essential nature of the primordial spontaneity. (See reference to *hun* (渾) line 7.)

cf: Zhuangzi chapter 6:
> 'The true men of old did not know how to be pleased that they were alive, did not know how to hate death, were neither glad to come forth nor reluctant to go in…' (A. C. Graham)

241. 形 若 槁 木 心 若 死 灰
    xing ruo gao mu xin ruo si hui

Their bodies are like dried wood, their hearts are like dead ashes.

They do not react with the body or the mind; there is no personal will or movement.

cf: Zhuangzi chapter 2:
> 'Can you really make the body like a withered tree and the mind like dead ashes?' (B. Watson)

242. 忘 其 五 藏 損 其 形 骸
wang qi wu zang sun qi xing hai

Having forgotten their five organs and destroyed their physical form,

243. 不 學 而 知 不 視 而 見
bu xue er zhi bu shi er jian

they do not study, yet they know; they do not look, yet they see;

cf: Laozi chapter 47:
'Therefore the sage knows without going, names without seeing and completes without doing a thing.' (R. G. Hendricks)

cf: Laozi chapter 81:
'He who has extensive knowledge is not a wise man.'
(Wing-tsit Chan)

244. 不 為 而 成 不 治 而 辯
bu wei er cheng bu zhi er bian

they do not act, yet they accomplish; they do not rule, yet they govern.

cf: Huainanzi chapter 9:
'The art of the ruler is to deal with things through non-action.'
(R. T. Ames)

cf: Laozi chapter 48:
'They do nothing and yet there's nothing left undone.'
(R. G. Hendricks)

245. 感 而 應 迫 而 動
gan er ying po er dong

They respond when stimulated, they move when pushed.

They are not motivated to act by their own will, but respond spontaneously and naturally from within. *Gan* (感) and *ying* (應) describe the principle of mutual resonance. They are the key theme explored in Huainanzi chapter 6. (cf: Huai Nan Tzu, Charles le Blanc.)

cf: Huainanzi chapter 1:
'The sage ...sinks and floats, rises and falls with the *dao*.'
(Ames and Lau)

246. 不 得 已 而 往 如 光 之 燿 如 景 之 放
bu de yi er wang ru guang zhi yao ru ying zhi fang
They cannot help but go aimlessly as a ray of light, like shadows cast.

cf: Zhuangzi chapter 2:
'Penumbra said to Shadow, "A little while ago you were walking and now you're standing still; a little while ago you were sitting and now you're standing up. Why this lack of independent action?"' (B. Watson)

247. 以 道 為 紃 有 待 而 然
yi dao wei xun you dai er ran
They take the *dao* as their law, awaiting its cue.

248. 抱 其 太 清 之 本 而 無 所 容 與 而 物 無 能 營
bao qi tai qing zhi ben er wu suo rong yu er wu wu neng ying
They embrace the root of the great purity and are not concerned with anyone, so nothing can trouble them.

249. 廓 怊 而 虛 清 靖 而 無 思 慮
kuo chang er xu qing jing er wu si lü
Expansive, vast and empty! Pure, tranquil and without thoughts

and cares.

250. 大 澤 焚 而 不 能 熱
da zhai fen er bu neng re
Huge marshes set alight cannot burn them;

251. 河 漢 涸 而 不 能 寒 也
he han he er bu neng han ye
rivers and streams ice over but cannot freeze them;

252. 大 雷 毀 山 而 不 能 驚 也
da lei hui shan er bu neng jing ye
great thunderstorms break down mountains but cannot frighten them;

253. 大 風 晦 日 而 不 能 傷 也
da feng hui ri er bu neng shang ye
great winds obscure the sun but cannot harm them.

254. 是 故 視 珍 寶 珠 玉 猶 石 礫 也
shi gu shi zhen bao zhu yu you shi li ye
Therefore they consider jewels such as pearls and jade as if they were gravel.

255. 視 至 尊 窮 寵 猶 行 客 也
shi zhi zun qiong chong you xing ke ye
They regard the highest dignitaries and those most favoured as travellers at the door.

256. 視 毛 嬙 西 施 猶 顙 醜 也
shi mao qiang xi shi you qi chou ye

They consider Mao Qiang and Xi Shi as ugly and deformed.

Mao Qiang and Xi Shu were the favourite concubines of King of Yue, regarded as great beauties.

257. 以 死 生 為 一 化
yi si sheng wei yi hua

They regard death and life as transformations within the One

258. 以 萬 物 為 一 方
yi wan wu wei yi fang

and the ten thousand beings as an aspect of the One.

259. 同 精 於 太 清 之 本 而 游 於 忽 區 之 旁
tong jing yu tai qing zhi ben er you yu hu ju zhi pang

They share essences with the root of the great purity, they roam about in the region of the indistinct.

260. 有 精 而 不 使 有 神 而 不 行
you jing er bu shi you shen er bu xing

They have essences but do not use them, they have spirits but do not activate them.

261. 契 大 渾 之 樸 而 立 至 清 之 中
qi da hun zhi pu er li zhi qing zhi zhong

They have a pact with the primal simplicity of the great chaos and they stand in the centre of the perfect purity.

Pu (樸), the uncarved block, is translated here as primal simplicity (see note to line 229).

262. 是 故 其 寢 不 夢 其 智 不 萌
　　　　shi gu qi qin bu meng qi zhi bu meng
Therefore their sleep is without dreams; their wisdom does not burst forth;

263. 其 魄 不 抑 其 魂 不 騰
　　　　qi po bu yi qi hun bu teng
their *po* do not sink and their *hun* do not rise.

The *hun* and *po* souls must intertwine to keep the *yin yang* balance necessary for life. The sinking of the *po* and the rising of the *hun* are a sign of potential disintegration, because on death the *po* sink down and return to earth, the *hun* rise and return to heaven. (See note to line 222)

264. 反 覆 終 始 不 知 其 端 緒
　　　　fan fu zhong shi bu zhi qi duan xu
They go back and forth between beginnings and endings not knowing their extremities and successions

Fan (反) to return, revert. cf: Laozi 40:
　　"Reversal" (*fan* 反)is the movement of the Tao.'
　　(R. G. Hendricks)

265. 甘 暝 太 宵 之 宅
　　　　gan ming tai xiao zhi zhai
They delight in closing their eyes in the abode of the great night

266. 而 覺 視 于 昭 昭 之 宇
er jue shi yu zhao zhao zhi yu
and they awaken and look around in the realm of the brilliant light

267. 休 息 于 無 委 曲 之 隅
xiu xi yu wu wei qu zhi yu
They rest and relax in a cornerless corner

268. 而 游 敖 于 無 形 埒 之 野
er you nao yu wu xing lie zhi ye
And roam to and fro in a wilderness without form

269. 居 而 無 容 處 而 無 所
ju er wu rong chu er wu suo
They dwell in a space that cannot contain, settle in a place that is nowhere;

270. 其 動 無 形 其 靜 無 體
qi dong wu xing qi jing wu ti
they move in the formless; are still in the bodyless

271. 存 而 若 亡 生 而 若 死
cun er ruo wang sheng er ruo si
They are present as if vanished and live as if dead

272. 出 入 無 間 役 使 鬼 神
chu ru wu jian yi shi gui shen
They enter and leave where there is no opening, use ghosts and spirits as servants

cf: Laozi chapter 43:
 'Only Nothing can enter into no-space' (J. C. Wu)

 'Only the least substantial thing can penetrate the seamless' (Ames and Hall)

Ghosts and spirits (*gui shen* 鬼 神) are the spirits of earth and heaven, and can be understood on many levels. They may refer to the souls of the dead, but are also mentioned in records of shamanic travel. Here the sage is at one with the spirits of heaven and earth and he may command them, since he participates in the power of the *dao*.

273. 淪 於 不 測 入 於 無 間 以 不 同 形 相 嬗 也
 lun yu bu ce ru yu wu jian yi bu tong xing xiang shan ye
They are engulfed by the unfathomable and enter into what has no opening, in order to be moulded into different forms

274. 終 始 若 環 莫 得 其 倫
 zhong shi ruo huan mo de qi lun
Endings and beginnings are like a circle, no one can grasp their succession

275. 此 精 神 之 所 以 能 登 假 於 道 也
 ci jing shen zhi suo yi neng deng jia yu dao ye
This is how the vital spirits are able to merge with the *dao*

276. 是 故 真 人 之 所 游 若 吹 呴 呼 吸 吐 故 內 新
 shi gu zhen ren zhi suo you ruo chui he hu xi tu gu nei xin
Therefore, the authentic men in their roamings, [do not let their hearts be disturbed] by puffing and blowing, inhaling and exhaling, expelling the old, taking in the new;

277. 熊 經 鳥 伸 鳧 浴 蝯 躩 鴟 視 虎 顧
xiong jing niao shen fu yu yuan jue chi shi hu gu
bear lumbering, bird stretching, duck ablutions, monkey jumping, owl gazing and tiger staring –

278. 是 養 形 之 人 也
shi yang xing zhi ren ye
all that is for men to nourish the body.

cf: Zhuangzi chapter 15:

> 'To pant, to puff, to hail, to sip, to spit out the old breath and draw in the new, practicing bear hangings, and bird-stretchings, longevity his only concern … the man who nourishes his body, who hopes to be as old as Peng tsu.' (B. Watson)

These exercises, derived from animal movements, are an ancient form of *dao yin,* as seen in the silk painting and texts of the beginning of the 2nd century BCE discovered in the Mawangdui tombs. In the Huainanzi, 'sitting quietly doing nothing' is contrasted with the gymnastics employed by those desiring longevity and using physical means to obtain it. Pengzi is the immortal who lived for 800 years. What is the value in being as old as Pengzi – when there is so much more to be!

279. 不 以 滑 心
bu yi gu xin
[do not let their hearts be disturbed]

Gu (滑), here pronounced *gu* and not *hua*, has the meaning of to disturb, to confuse. For clearer understanding, this line of the text is placed within line 276 in the translation.

280. 使 神 滔 蕩 而 不 失 其 充
shi shen tao dang er bu shi qi chong

Even if they use their spirits until they overflow, they do not lose their fullness.

Because they understand, have embodied and act according to the natural rhythms of life, (*jie* 節) they are not exhausted. (cf: Laozi chapters 4, 5, 6.)

281. 日 夜 無 傷 而 與 物 為 春
ri ye wu shang er yu wu wei chun

They are unharmed day and night and are the spring for beings.

Spring is the source of the constant renewal of life. As springtime gives life to all of nature, authentic men give life to the world. This is a recurring theme in the Zhuangzi.

282. 則 是 合 而 生 時 於 心 也
ze shi he er sheng shi yu xin ye

Then there is unity and timeliness is generated in the heart.

It is important to be in tune with the present moment and to respond appropriately. Season and time are translations of the same character *shi* (時).

cf: Huainanzi chapter 1,
'The right moment becomes the wrong before one can take a breath. One who acts too soon anticipates the opportunity, and one who acts too late gets left behind.' (Ames and Lau)

283. 且 人 有 戒 形 而 無 損 於 心
qie ren you jie xing er wu sun yu xin

The human body is prepared and the heart not weakened.

284. 有 綴 宅 而 無 耗 精
you zhui zhai er wu hao jing

From dwelling place to dwelling place, the essences are not exhausted.

'Dwelling place' refers to the body. The body is the dwelling place of the *jing shen*, which are able to move from physical form to physical form. Death is a transformation, as seen in lines 203, 257, 258.

285. 夫 癩 者 趨 不 變 狂 者 形 不 虧
fu lai zhe qu bu bian kuang zhe xing bu kui

The leper's pace is not changed and the body of a madman is not impaired.

The body may be damaged but the spirits are not affected.

286. 神 將 有 所 遠 徙 孰 暇 知 其 所 為
shen jiang you suo yuan xi shu xia zhi qi suo wei

But if their spirits flee far away who knows what will happen?

If the spirits are affected no one knows what will happen to the body.

cf: Huainanzi chapter 1:
    'Now, the madman is unable to avoid the hazards of fire...'
    (Ames and Lau)

287. 故 形 有 摩 而 神 未 嘗 化 者
gu xing you mo er shen wei chang hua zhe
So the body wears out, but the spirits are not subject to transformation.

288. 以 不 化 應 化
yi bu hua ying hua
Because they are not transformed, they resonate with all transformations.

Only pure spirits are not transformed, they follow freely the way of the world, companions of the *dao*. Because such spirits are beyond transformation they resonate with any form of life which is taken. A human being is able to attract such pure spirits and become one with them.

289. 千 變 萬 抮 而 未 始 有 極
qian bian wan zhen er wei shi you ji
A thousand changes and ten thousand twists and turns – and not even the beginning of their limit.

290. 化 者 復 歸 於 無 形 也
hua zhe fu gui yu wu xing ye
That which is transformed returns and reverts to the formless.

291. 不 化 者 與 天 地 俱 生 也
bu hua zhe yu tian di ju sheng ye
That which is not transformed shares all life with heaven and earth.

292. 夫 木 之 死 也 青 青 去 之 也
fu mu zhi si ye qing qing qu zhi ye
A tree dies when the green vitality departs.

Qing (青) is the colour of the renewing of life seen in springtime.

293. 夫 使 木 生 者 豈 木 也
fu shi mu sheng zhe qi mu ye
So how could it be that what makes a tree alive is the tree itself?

294. 猶 充 形 者 之 非 形 也
you chong xing zhe zhi fei xing ye
In the same way, that which gives the body its fullness is not the body itself.

295. 故 生 生 者 未 嘗 死 也 其 所 生 則 死 矣
gu sheng sheng zhe wei chang si ye qi suo sheng ze si yi
Therefore, that which generates life never dies, but that which is given life dies.

296. 化 物 者 未 嘗 化 也 其 所 化 則 化 矣
hua wu zhe wei chang hua ye qi suo hua ze hua yi
That which transforms beings is never transformed; it is that which is transformed which is transformed.

297. 輕 天 下 則 神 無 累 矣
qing tian xia ze shen wu lei yi
Giving no importance to the world, the spirits are not entangled

298. 細 萬 物 則 心 不 惑 矣
xi wan wu ze xin bu huo yi
Making little of the ten thousand beings, the heart is not deluded

299. 齊 死 生 則 志 不 懾 矣
qi si sheng ze zhi bu zhe yi
Considering life and death as equal, the will is not shaken.

(See note to line 239)

300. 同 變 化 則 明 不 眩 矣
tong bian hua ze ming bu xuan yi
Regarding all change and transformation as the same, clarity is not obscured.

'Clarity (*ming* 明) is the light inherent in the spirits of heaven; the destiny or fulfilment of a human being is to allow this light to illuminate the heart/mind, in order to be aware of things as they are and to act accordingly.' (E. Rochat de la Vallée)

SELECTED BIBLIOGRAPHY

SELECTED BIBLIOGRAPHY

Ames, Roger T., *The Art of Rulership: A Study of Ancient Chinese Political Thought.* (Honolulu: University of Hawaii Press, 1983)

Ames, Roger T. and David L. Hall, *Dao De Jing: 'Making This Life Significant'.* (New York: Ballantine Books, 2003)

Ames, Roger T. and D. C. Lau, *Yuan Dao: Tracing Dao to Its Source.* (New York: Ballantine Books, 1998)

Chan, Wing-tsit, *A Source Book in Chinese Philosophy.* (Princeton: Princeton University Press, 1963) Graham, A. C., *Chuang-Tzu The Inner Chapters.* (London: George Allen & Unwin, 1981)

Graham, A. C., *The Book of Lieh Tzu.* (London: John Murray, 1960)

Harper, Donald, *Early Chinese Medical Literature: The Mawangdui Medical Manuscripts.* (The Sir Henry Wellcome Asian Series. Kegan Paul International, 1998)

Hendricks, Robert G., *Lao-Tzu Te-Tao Ching: a new translation based upon the recently discovered Ma-wang-tui texts.* (New York: Ballantine Books, 1989)

Knoblock, John, and Jeremy Riegel, *Lüshi Chunqui, The Annals of Lü Buwei: A Complete Translation and Study.* (Stanford: Stanford University Press, 2000)

Larre, Claude, *The Way of Heaven.* (Cambridge: Monkey Press, 1994)

Larre, Claude and Elisabeth Rochat de la Vallée, *La Bannière: pour une dame chinoise allant en paradis.* (Paris: Desclée De Brouwer, 1995)

Larre, Claude and Elisabeth Rochat de la Vallée, *The Heart in Lingshu chapter 8.* (London: Monkey Press, 2000)

Larre, Claude and Elisabeth Rochat de la Vallée, *The Extraordinary Fu*. (London: Monkey Press, 2003)

Larre, Claude and Elisabeth Rochat de la Vallée, *The Secret Treatise of the Spiritual Orchid*. (London: Monkey Press, 2003)

Larre, Claude, Isabelle Robinet, Elisabeth Rochat de la Vallée, *Les Grands Traités du Huainan Zi*. (Paris: Le Cerf, 1993)

Lau, D. C., *Lao Tzu* (London: Penguin Books 1963)

Le Blanc, Charles, *Huai Nan Tzu – Philosophical Synthesis in Early Han Thought*. (Hong Kong: Hong Kong University Press, 1985)

Legge, James, *The Sacred Books of the East: The Texts of Confucianism*. (Oxford: Oxford University Books, 1885)

Liu Wendian: *Huai Nan Hong Lie Ji Jie,* (Shanghai: Shangwu, 1923; Taipei reprint, 1968.)

Lynn, Richard John, *Tao-te Ching: A New Translation of Laozi as interpreted by Wang Bi*. (New York: Columbia University Press, 1999)

Major, John S., *Heaven And Earth In Early Han Thought: Chapters Three, Four and Five of Huainanzi*. (Albany: State University of New York Press, 1993)

Murray, Judson B., *A Study Of Yaolüe, 'A Summary of Essentials': Understanding the Huainanzi from the Point of View of the Author of the Postface*. (Early China 29, 2004)

Rochat de la Vallée, Elisabeth, *La vie, la médecine et la sagesse*. (Paris: Le Cerf, 2005)

Rochat de la Vallée, Elisabeth, *Yin Yang in Classical Texts*. (London: Monkey Press, 2006)

Rochat de la Vallée, Elisabeth, *Pregnancy and Gestation.* (London: Monkey Press, 2007)

Rochat de la Vallée, Elisabeth, *Wu Xing: the five elements in Chinese classical texts.* (London: Monkey Press, 2009)

Roth, Harold D., *Original Tao: Inward Training (Nei-yeh) and the Foundations of Taoist Mysticism.* (New York: Columbia University Press, 1999)

Watson, Burton, *The Complete Works of Chuang Tzu.* (New York: Columbia University Press, 1968)

Wu, John C. H., *Lao Tzu Tao Teh Ching.* (New York: St John's University Press, 1961)